TEACHING ENGLISH LEARNERS

TEACHER'S TOOLKIT SERIES

1

Teaching for Success:
Developing Your Teacher Identity in Today's Classroom
Brad Olsen (UC–Santa Cruz)

2

Teaching English Learners:
Fostering Language and the Democratic Experience
Kip Téllez (UC–Santa Cruz)

3

Teaching Without Bells: What We Can Learn
from Powerful Practice in Small Schools
Joey Feldman (New Haven Unified School District)

4

Leading from the Inside Out:
Expanded Roles for Teachers in Equitable Schools
W. Norton Grubb and Lynda Tredway
(UC–Berkeley)

5

Teaching Toward Democracy:
Educators as Agents of Change
William Ayers (U of Ill–Chicago), Kevin Kumashiro (U of Ill–Chicago),
Erica Meiners (Northeastern Illinois University),
Therese Quinn (The Art Institute of Chicago), and David Stovall (U of Ill–Chicago)

6

Making a Difference:
Developing Meaningful Careers in Education
Karen Hunter Quartz (UCLA), Brad Olsen (UC–Santa Cruz),
Lauren Anderson (UCLA), and Kimberly Barraza Lyons (UCLA)

TEACHING ENGLISH LEARNERS

Fostering Language and
the Democratic Experience

Kip Téllez

TEACHER'S TOOLKIT SERIES

Paradigm Publishers
Boulder · London

Copyright © 2010 Paradigm Publishers

Published in the United States by Paradigm Publishers, 2845 Wilderness Place, Suite 200, Boulder, CO 80301 USA.

Paradigm Publishers is the trade name of Birkenkamp & Company, LLC, Dean Birkenkamp, President and Publisher.

Library of Congress Cataloging-in-Publication Data

Téllez, Kip.
    Teaching English learners : fostering language and the democratic experience / Kip Téllez.
        p. cm. — (Teacher's toolkit series)
    Includes bibliographical references and index.
    ISBN 978-1-59451-830-0 (pbk. : alk. paper)
    1. English language—Study and teaching—Foreign speakers. 2. English language—United States. 3. Language and languages—United States. I. Title.
    PE1128.A2T45123 2010
    428.2'4—dc22

                                    2009036145

Printed and bound in the United States of America on acid-free paper that meets the standards of the American National Standard for Permanence of Paper for Printed Library Materials.

Designed by Cynthia Young.
Typeset by Mulberry Tree Enterprises.

14 13 12 11 10   1 2 3 4 5

I dedicate this book to my mother, Kay, whose teaching is ongoing.

CONTENTS

Series Foreword   ix

Preface and Acknowledgments   xvii

1 ELD: When Language, Geopolitics, Democracy,
   and Culture Merge   1

2 English-Language Learners in the United States:
   A Statistical and Biographical Portrait   29

3 Language Acquisition or Learning?   61

4 Bilingual Education, ELD, and the Debate   85

5 Language Teaching: Methods Less Familiar   109

6 The ELD Teacher: A Special Psychology   131

7 Teaching ELLs and the Democratic Ideal   145

References   163

Index   173

About the Author   182

SERIES FOREWORD

THIS TEACHER'S TOOLKIT series is a set of six related books written for prospective, new, and experienced teachers who are committed to students and families, who conceive of themselves as agents of democratic change, and who are eager to think more deeply, more broadly, and more practically about their work in education. All six books succinctly link theory with practice, present extended arguments for improving education, and wrap their discussions around successful examples of the topics in question.

Although each book is its own resource, the books in the Toolkit series share some common views about teaching. For one, all of the books treat teachers not as mere deliverers of curriculum but as active, three-dimensional professionals capable of diagnosing student learning, developing powerful educational experiences, assessing and adjusting student learning, and forming productive relationships with children and adults in schools. Another view all of the books share is that teaching is hard work that is among the most important kinds of work any society requires. My grandmother used to say that no society can survive without farmers or teachers. I think that is still true. Teaching is undeniably difficult work, but it is also frequently enjoyable work because it is so challenging, meaningful, and success oriented. These books are for teachers who have accepted the challenges of teaching because they relish the satisfaction of the work, they enjoy helping young people grow, and they know that quality education is necessary for the health of our world.

A third commonality about teaching among these books is their shared presumption that teachers are always looking for ways to improve. Teaching is a profession in which one enters as a novice, develops expertise over time, and continues to grow and change throughout the whole of one's career. The Toolkit books are written for teachers at multiple points in their career cycle: Beginning teachers will learn new ways to think about learning, students, and what it means to become a successful educator. Early- and middle-career teachers can reflect on their own practice in light of the ideas, strategies, and stories of these books—and they can use the books to deepen and broaden their future work. Veteran teachers can see themselves and their varied experiences inside the perspectives of the books, as well as figure out how they can continue to challenge themselves and their students—and perhaps take on other kinds of education work such as mentoring newer teachers, advocating for students on a broader stage, or writing about their own teaching. No matter where readers are in their education careers, these books offer powerful learning and useful opportunities for professional reflection.

The six books are sequenced to loosely follow both the career cycle of teaching and the fact that, as teachers progress, they often widen their sphere of influence. Book 1 in the series is *Teaching for Success: Developing Your Teacher Identity in Today's Classroom* by Brad Olsen. This book focuses on the processes of "becoming a teacher" and explores how to teach well in this contemporary age. Wrapping its conversations about teacher development around the core concept of teacher identity, the book offers its own teacher learning experience: how to recognize, adjust, and maximize the many ways your personal self and your professional self become integrated in your teaching work.

Book 2, *Teaching English Learners: Fostering Language and the Democratic Experience*, by Kip Téllez, focuses on what teachers can do in their classrooms in order to better understand and more effectively teach English learners. Drawing from research and experience not only on learning and teaching but also on culture, language, immigration, and contemporary politics, Téllez offers a unique guide for use by U.S. teachers interested in deeply and compassionately supporting the growth of students whose native language is not English.

Book 3 in the series is *Teaching Without Bells: What We Can Learn from Powerful Instruction in Small Schools* by Joey Feldman. This book offers a valuable look at how teaching and learning are fundamentally influenced by school size. The book's premise is that student and teacher experiences in education are direct functions of their school's size (and its accompanying influence on how schools are organized). Focusing on challenges and benefits of teaching in small high schools, Feldman's book helps readers consider where they might want to teach and—no matter the size of their school site—how they can teach well by maximizing lessons from the small schools movement.

Book 4, *Leading from the Inside Out: Expanded Roles for Teachers in Equitable Schools*, by Norton Grubb and Lynda Tredway, opens up the professional world of the teacher by offering new ways to think about school reform from the vantage point of the teacher. The authors make a compelling case for teachers as the key ingredient in education re-form and schools as the lever for democratic educational change. Pre-senting a blueprint for a new kind of school in which teachers are not only classroom instructors but education reformers as well, Grubb and Tredway illustrate why we have the schools we have today and how broad-minded teachers can transform them into successful schools for tomorrow.

Book 5, *Teaching Toward Democracy: Educators as Agents of Change,* by William Ayers, Kevin Kumashiro, Erica Meiners, Therese Quinn, and David Stovall, also considers teachers as agents of change on a broader scale. The authors share their ideas about how teachers can better humanize schooling for students, combat some of the current failings of market models of education, and extend their teaching work past the school day and outside the school walls. Their book invites readers into a view of education through the eyes of students, and it provides thoughtful strategies to enact teaching for social justice as not just a popular slogan but as an authentic focus on human rights and social equity for all.

And, to close out the series, Book 6, *Making a Difference: Develop-ing Meaningful Careers in Education*, by Karen Hunter Quartz, Brad Olsen, Lauren Anderson, and Kimberly Barraza Lyons, looks at whole careers in education. This book examines the dynamic lives and work of several educators in Los Angeles and investigates why teachers stay in the classroom or shift to other kinds of education roles, such as school administrator, curriculum coordinator, or teacher mentor. The book unpacks the sometimes maddening complexity of the teaching profession and offers a roadmap for how teachers can, themselves, re-main challenged and satisfied as educators without relaxing their com-mitments to students.

There are different approaches to reading the books in this series. One way is to consider the whole series as a coherent set of sequenced conversations about teaching. In this manner, you might read the books one at a time, all the way through, inserting yourself into the text of the books: Do the stories and experiences in the books ring true for you? How will you use these books to improve your practice, broaden your influence, and deepen your professional satisfaction? You might imag-ine, as you read the books this way, that you are sitting in a room with the authors—listening to their ideas, questioning them, actively engag-ing with their arguments, or talking back to the text when necessary.

Or perhaps you might use these books as textbooks—as thoughtful primers on selected topics that interest you. In this manner, you might pick and choose particular chapters to study: Which specific ideas will you implement in your teaching tomorrow? Are there further readings or key resources that you will hunt down and look at on your own? What concrete activities will you try out? Write notes in the margins of the books and return to the chapters regularly. Photocopy single pages (not whole chapters, please!) to share with peers. Use the books as you plan lessons or design curricula. Engage with the reflection questions at the end of each book's chapters. You will find occasionally in the margins cross-references on specific topics to other books in the series. When you read "Cross-Reference, See Book 2 …" you can use the numbered list of titles on p. ii to correlate each reference to the in-tended book.

Or, you may pick some of the books to read collectively with other educators—maybe with your teacher education cohort, or as a group of teachers working with a mentor, or perhaps as part of a teacher inquiry group that you set up with colleagues. Group discussion of these books allows their arguments, perspectives, and examples to prompt your own collective reflection and professional growth: What themes from the books call out to you? What points might you disagree with? How might different educators among you interpret parts of these books in different, perhaps competing, ways? How can these books inspire you to create specific collaborative projects or teacher networks at your school site? You may find the reflection questions at the end of each chapter particularly useful for group conversation.

This series of books is called the "Teacher's Toolkit," but maybe, for some, the idea of a *toolkit* for teachers may not, at first glance, be apt. Picturing a toolkit could conjure images of a steel toolbox or super-hero's belt full of hardware for educators—a diagnostic screwdriver, the clawhammer of homework, a set of precision wrenches for adjusting student learning on the fly. Such images are, well, just too instrumental. They risk suggesting that teaching is mechanical or automatic, or that what good educators do is select utensils from their box to apply when needed. That doesn't describe the kind of teaching I know and love. It erroneously suggests that students are to be fastened with bolts or hammered into obedience, or that learning is gut-wrenchingly rigid. And, to my mind, such a view treats teachers as technicians trained by rote, using tools given to them by others, following directions written on the outside of the box.

Instead, the authors of these books conceive of education as less fixed, more fluid, less finished, more uncertain, and certainly far more complicated than anything for which traditional tools would work. These authors—based on their own years of experience as classroom teachers, educational researchers, school administrators, and university professors—view education similarly to educational philosopher John Dewey when, in 1934, he wrote:

> About 40 years ago, a new idea dawned in education. Educators began to see that education should parallel life, that the school should repro-duce the child's world. In this new type of education the child, instead of the curriculum, became the centre of interest, and since the child is active, changing, creative—education ceased to be static, [and] became dynamic and creative in response to the needs of the child.[1]

Like Dewey, I understand teaching and learning to be context-specific, highly creative, dynamically student-centered activities that are as complicated and multifaceted as life itself. And just as important.

So let's reimagine the analogy of a teacher's toolkit. A *toolkit* for teach-ers could instead be a metaphor for a thoughtful, useful, provocative bundle of perspectives, theories, and approaches for teachers—a set of lively teaching discussions written by different authors who share some common ground. This bundle would empathize with teachers since its authors are all teachers, as well as education researchers and writers: they know both how difficult and how rewarding teaching can be. But it would also exhort teachers not to fall down on the job—not to shirk their work, make excuses, or lessen their resolve to support students.

The bundle of teaching conversations could share stories from the classroom that reveal teaching to be kaleidoscopic: made up of thousands of shifting views, hundreds of competing relations, and dozens of different ways to succeed with children. The stories would reveal how to be a great teacher and why doing so is so damned important. The bundle of ideas and perspectives would include actual examples of good teaching, lesson ideas, and lots of research tidbits useful for prospective and practicing educators. Yes, that could be a toolkit I would want to own. It would be a kit full of thoughtful perspectives, research summaries, wisdom of practice, and impassioned words of advice from handpicked educationalists. An "idea kit," really. A boxed set of thoughtful primers on how to teach well for social change in the current global climate.

John Dewey famously built up binaries in his writing—teaching is either this or that; students learn in this way but not in that way—only to collapse the binary in the end and suggest that education is too complicated for easy contradictions. So I'll take a page from Dewey's playbook and attempt the same. Maybe we can consider this book series as not an either/or. Not as *either* a box of teaching instruments *or* a collection of thoughtful conversations about education, but as both: a set of tangible strategies for teachers to make their own and a loosely bundled collection of professional arguments for use by educators in order to think for themselves, but in deeper and newer ways than before. That's the way that I prefer to envision this teacher's toolkit.

No matter how you choose to make use of the books in the Teacher's Toolkit, it is our sincere hope that you will find value in them. We have tried to make them accessible, conversational, substantive, and succinct. We all believe that teaching is a fundamentally important profession, and, if this world is to improve and grow, it will be because our teachers can help future generations to become wise, creative, and critical thinkers who put their ideas into action toward improving the societies they will inherit. You are an essential part of that human process.

—Brad Olsen
University of California, Santa Cruz

NOTE

1. Dewey, J. 1934. "Tomorrow May Be Too Late: Save the Schools Now." Reprinted in J. Boydston (ed.), *John Dewey: The Later Works, 1925–1953: 1933–1934, Vol. 9* (Carbondale: Southern Illinois University Press, 1986), 386.

PREFACE AND ACKNOWLEDGMENTS

THIS BOOK EXAMINES the teaching of English-language learners (ELLs) by exploring topics not typically covered in theory or methods textbooks. For instance, methods texts in English-language development (ELD) commonly draw readers through well-known strategies such as the audiolingual method. This book, by contrast, focuses attention on how music can advance language skills. Further, the book looks broadly at the sociocultural implications of ELD, examining in depth the role of the teacher in introducing students to both a new language and a new society. A broad description of ELLs is also included. Who are ELLs now, and who might they be in the future? The context in this section, like the context in the remainder of the book, focuses attention on ELLs in the United States. With regard to the study of language itself, the book offers again some alternative views of language and what teachers should know about it. While reviewing common theories of first-language acquisition (e.g., Chomsky, Clark), the book also examines anthropological and neuroscience evidence for research and theories that can inform teachers' knowledge. First-language theories are then linked to second-language considerations, again with linkages to teaching. Finally, I draw upon progressive pragmatic philosophy (Dewey, Addams, and Rorty) to help readers understand the lineage of educators they have joined (or will join). My hope in the final chapter is to offer information, inspiration, and sustenance for ELD teachers. I endeavor to help them understand their role as agents of our democratic ideals as they work with students whose personal and family histories are often filled with resignation, oppression, or both. Teachers are students' primary hope-givers.

ACKNOWLEDGMENTS

I would like to thank my teachers and wonderful colleagues, both past and present (in no particular order), from whom I've learned about language, languages, and language teaching: John Regan, Mary Poplin, Judith Walker de Felix, Sylvia Cavazos Peña, Hersh Waxman, Yolanda Padrón, Mark Dressman, Cindy Pease-Alvarez, George Bunch, Judit Moschkovich, Bill Johnston, Brian Morgan, Kimberly Johnson, and many, many students too numerous to mention. My UCSC colleague Brad Olsen's clear vision for the book series helped me stick to the story. Dean Birkenkamp and the wonderful team at Paradigm made the editing process easy. A special thanks goes to Angela Thompson, whose careful editing and suggestions allowed me to focus on the book's larger purpose. Finally, I thank my family, Sarah, Carmen, and Catrina, who, on occasion, allow me to use my expressive language capacities in the form of self-styled songs, often sung at a needlessly high volume.

- The Power of Labels
- The Promise and Challenge of Teaching English
- Are ELD Teachers Up for the Challenge?
- Language, Geopolitics, Democracy, and Culture

CHAPTER ONE

ELD

When Language, Geopolitics, Democracy, and Culture Merge

I F TEACHING IS THE unlocking of doors, then teaching English to immigrant children and youth is the making of keys. For better or worse, English has become the "koiné," the *lingua franca*, of the world, so when teachers help a student master this language, they are helping him or her to share in a global conversation on business, popular culture, and science, among many other topics.

English, with its irritating irregularities, its capacity for ensnaring the words of other languages and making them its own, and its insouciant mix of Greek and Latin, has become the most learned language in the world. And teachers have leaped at the opportunity to help students learn it. Yet in our zeal to teach English to a motivated world of learners, we may have underestimated some unwanted side effects, such as the loss of our students' native languages. Still, we have an obligation to own up to the power-tipping consequences of our work, and at the same time recognize our responsibility to respect and

In linguistics, a koiné language ("common language" in Greek) is a standard language or dialect that has arisen as a result of contact between two mutually intelligible varieties. A lingua franca (from Italian, literally meaning "Frankish language") is a language systematically used to communicate between persons not sharing a mother tongue, in particular when it is a third language, distinct from both persons' mother tongues.

nurture our students' native languages and cultures. But there is no doubt: speaking English alters *everything* for our learners.

THE POWER OF LABELS

As we begin this book, we must come to terms, quite literally, before moving on. I must admit that beginning a book with definitions belies everything I know about good pedagogy and writing, and yet I cannot escape the overwhelming urge to lay out a common set of terms, acronyms, and other nominal challenges before exploring the broader themes. Every professional field has its own vocabulary and shorthand, primarily designed for efficiency and accuracy. Acronyms can, of course, serve to create an inside and outside class, especially when they are short for common terms that anyone would know and thereby invented only to obfuscate. Like many educational endeavors, the field of English teaching is replete with acronyms, subtle distinctions known only to insiders, and complex terms that fairly reflect complex language teaching processes. In order to determine what language we need to make this book accessible, I want to devote some space to considering the implications of several of the common terms and acronyms that will be used.

We first need a common term to describe the "teaching of English to nonnative speakers in the U.S. context," which is clearly too long and cumbersome to use repeatedly. If this book were being published twenty years ago, the most likely term to use would have been *English as a second language,* or ESL. This term has fallen out of favor for two reasons: (1) a small but growing number of students are not learning English as a second language but perhaps as a third or even fourth; and (2) some outsiders to the field incorrectly assumed that the word *second* somehow implied that English was not as highly valued as the students' native languages. Next, we could take a very simple strategy and call it *English teaching,* but this term also has two primary problems: (1) secondary teachers of English justifiably call what they do "English teaching," and (2) we can argue that all teachers, especially elementary teachers, teach English, whether or not they have students who are learning English as an additional language. In place of these terms, I prefer *English-language development,* or ELD. For simplicity's sake, all the other terms for English teaching to nonnative speakers, whether the purpose is specially designed academic instruction in English (SDAIE) or what is sometimes called structured English immersion (SEI), are all under the ELD umbrella in my usage. *I believe that this phrase (and its acronym) indicates that we are talking about teaching English as a specific language but also recognizing it as a developmental process. Of course, no one has mastered the English language entirely, so we are all in the process of learning our language(s), but the implication is on growth in language use.* In the wider world of language teaching (and at times in this book) it is common to hear the term *second-language teaching,* or L2. This term is useful when we are talking about those general strategies of teaching that seem to work in all second-language settings, whether the student is learning French in a U.S. high school or studying English in a Korean "cram" school.

What about the students themselves? What term might best be used in a book such as this one? There are several options before us, but I would like to eliminate

Focus point

Think for a moment: What are some acronyms used in your school to describe the processes of teaching, learning, and curriculum development? In what ways are those terms sometimes misinterpreted or misused?

one at the outset. In the United States it is still irritatingly common to hear some educators refer to a student as "LEP," or limited English proficient. This federal designation sounds ugly ("leper" or "lip") and, more important, points our attention to what the student does *not* know. Like many ELD educators, I have tried to support other, more positive terms. In one article (Téllez 1998), I argued that our students were best referred to as "emerging bilinguals," a term that I believe both emphasizes the developmental aspect of teaching and learning, and made clear that all students have a native language and are now gaining a new one. After a few years of trying to convince my graduate students and colleagues to adopt the "emerging bilingual" label, I gave up. Although I still think my term has merit and others have recently used one similar (García, Kleifgen, and Falchi 2008), I have acceded to convention on this score and now use *English-language learner,* or ELL. Even this term is not without its own troubles, however; importantly, it neither makes mention of the student's native language nor reflects a developmental process. Nevertheless, this term is by far the most commonly used today to describe students who are learning English as a new language.

The terms that refer to ethnic or racial categories raise even knottier troubles than those used for language learners. I do not expect all readers to agree with my terminology, but I feel compelled to explain my thinking. As will become clear, the vast majority of ELLs in the United States are either from Mexico or have parents (or grandparents) from Mexico; therefore, these are the ELLs most commonly discussed in the book. The term *His-*

panic might work to describe them, but it suggests a relation to either the Spanish language or to Spain, neither of which is necessarily true for ELLs whose cultural heritage lies in Mexico. Although the term *Hispanic* is used frequently in certain parts of the country (e.g., Texas) and as a common descriptor in government use, I believe that *Mexican-descent* (for more recent immigrants) or *Mexican American* (for those who were born in the United States) is better. *Latino/a* is used when describing all those ELLs whose native language is Spanish and whose cultural backgrounds may extend beyond Mexico (e.g., El Salvador, Nicaragua).

Another example is the label *Asian American,* which could include people from India, Laos, China, Indonesia, and the Philippines, and many others all grouped together as if they were the same. To my mind, the term *Asian American* is almost useless. To consider an ELL whose cultural background is Laotian alongside one whose heritage is Taiwanese makes little sense. Consequently, I will use terms to reflect the country of origin (e.g., *Vietnamese-descent* or *Vietnamese American*) rather than the general and imprecise term *Asian American.*

As teachers, we do care about the names we give to what we do and the students with whom we work. Of course, merely having labels does not suggest action. Calling a student an ELL says nothing about the student's native language proficiency, her learning needs, or how we should go about teaching her. Merely saying that I am an ELD teacher indicates nothing about the methods I use or the curriculum I promote. These discussions are forthcoming.

THE PROMISE AND CHALLENGE OF TEACHING ENGLISH

Teaching ELD is often considered challenging work, but for the right kind of teacher, it is the only work imaginable. Those of us who teach ELD are fortunate because we

Those of us who teach ELD are fortunate because we find learning *about* language and languages compelling.

find learning *about* language and languages compelling. We may also consider ourselves fortunate because we welcome and find rewards in teaching the world's refugees as well as helping students and their families adjust to their lives in a new country, where novel freedoms create both opportunities and tensions. Finally, we as ELD teachers are comfortable acquiring new cultures; we do not mind making the inevitable mistakes and silly assumptions when confronted with a people unlike ourselves. But not all teachers are willing to take on these challenges.

ARE ELD TEACHERS UP FOR THE CHALLENGE?

The data suggest that many teachers of ELLs are unsure of their capacities. Over half of the teachers serving language learners report that they are underprepared to teach their ELLs (Alexander, Heaviside, and Farris 1999; Gándara et al. 2003). Why do so many ELD teachers believe themselves to be underprepared for the crucial work of teaching language? One very obvious reason is that when teachers lose their ability to communicate through language, they have lost their most important instructional tool. And if we know anything about teaching, it is that teachers talk, and they depend on the fact that students can understand the messages they send. We might offer up a critique of teachers at this point, saying that they talk too much, but when they lose their primary mode of communication they no doubt feel lost.

A second reason why teachers might feel underprepared for their ELLs is that their preparation program has somehow failed them. But to blame teacher education entirely for failing to prepare teachers for ELLs is somewhat unfair, given the myriad knowledge and skills such preparation programs must impart. We must also recognize that many teachers were prepared in an era of far fewer ELLs. For instance, Alabama, Indiana, Kentucky, Nebraska, North Carolina, South Carolina, and

Tennessee have all experienced at least a 300 percent increase in the number of ELLs from 1995 to 2005. North Carolina had fewer than 20,000 ELLs in 1995; its ELL population now exceeds 70,000. Many veteran teachers were hired at a time when few ELLs attended their schools, and they are struggling to learn strategies that work.

Third, it may be that various schooling organizations, such as districts or states, have failed to provide resources to support ELD teachers in their work (Téllez and Waxman 2006). Teachers are commonly critical of the "in-service" programs offered by districts, but limited resources make genuine and lasting professional development a challenge.

These reasons, as well as many others, play a role in making ELD the complex instructional endeavor it is. Nevertheless, I believe that although ELD teaching is challenging work, it is exactly the proper work for a teacher who sees how working with ELLs links teachers to issues that resonate well inside and outside the classroom. ELD teachers must be ready and able to develop knowledge and even interests in four broad arenas of knowledge, all of which go well beyond what "other" teachers must know.

LANGUAGE, GEOPOLITICS, DEMOCRACY, AND CULTURE

Language

ELD holds an obvious attraction for those of us who are compelled to learn more *about* language and languages, not only those who want to learn *different* languages, such as French or Finnish. Although it is certainly true that many who are drawn to ELD are bilingual or trilingual—or have mastered even more than four languages to some degree—the work of the ELD teacher is about taking each and every student and his native language and helping him to learn English. And for this work, we must possess a unique mixture of knowledge and skills. First, ELD teachers must know English very well. Its rules, structure, and lexicon are required features of anyone who hopes to be a model for ELLs. Second, they must have a capacity for understanding the structure and forms of lots of different languages. Naturally, any ELD teacher should have the experience of learning at least one other language, perhaps not to the point of full proficiency in that language but certainly to the point of knowing how it feels to be a language learner. Merely knowing another language, however, is insufficient to be an effective ELD instructor. It is a common fallacy that simply being bilingual in English and another language, especially if it is the native language of the students, is an instant qualification to teach ELD. *Knowing the language of the students can be very useful, but merely having learned two languages can encourage teachers to assume that each student's language learning experience will mirror their own. This is a dangerous assumption. Not only do ELLs have widely different linguistic, cultural, and schooling backgrounds, but to generalize from a data point of one (the teacher) to all students is a fundamental flaw in logic.*

Focus point

ELD teachers who are fascinated by the range of human languages can use the field to their advantage. In my view, the finest and most satisfied ELD teachers are those who not only know English and a second language well, but who are equally interested in learning the structure of many different languages. Teachers who can focus on how languages do their work, how languages serve their purposes of human communication and individual

When we consider those who speak multiple languages, we refer to one who speaks more than two languages as a "polyglot." When we consider cultures or societies that routinely use more than one language, we refer to it as "multiglossic" (Fishman 1980).

thought, and how ELLs come to understand the relationship between their native and new languages are better prepared to address the challenges brought by all the
possible languages spoken by students. For instance,
some teachers, upon inviting a new ELL to the class who
speaks a language they do not know, take it upon themselves to study the nature and structure of the student's
native language. They may ask: How does the syntax of
this language operate? Does this language have prefixes?
How is verb tense marked? Such an investigation does
not necessarily mean learning to speak the unfamiliar
language with great proficiency, which is an unlikely
achievement.

In just one year I taught ten- and eleven-year-old
ELLs whose native languages included Spanish, Vietnamese, Egyptian Arabic, Samoan, and Tagalog. Although it is not impossible to learn all these languages, I
could not practically become proficient in them all, especially in the time frame of one school year. In place of
learning to speak each language (I do speak functional
Spanish and am approaching intermediate status in Vietnamese), I studied the forms of the language (e.g.,
Schachter and Otanes 1972), trying to understand how
they relate to English. Seeking answers to these questions
serves as powerful motivation for the professional ELD
teacher who enjoys languages, both learning them and
taking them apart to see how they work.

ELD teachers are also fascinated by the ways we communicate without using language. How does the teacher
help to integrate a new student in the classroom if her
language is unknown to anyone at the school? In a fascinating paradox, ELD teachers must, of course, understand how learning occurs using language, but also how
it could happen without it. Making ideas accessible to
learners at all levels of English development requires us
to consider language-reduced teaching strategies. Images,
video, and graphical representations of knowledge are
fundamental to promoting content knowledge. This is

Think for a moment: What are some nonverbal ways of communicating between humans? Between animals?

also why ELD teachers are interested in gestures and other nonverbal ways of communicating.

WHAT IS LANGUAGE? A devotion to understanding language also includes the realization that language is the primary tool for learning about the world. The well-known linguist Michael Halliday suggests a three-part understanding of language, advising that educators reconsider the concept of "language acquisition," a point we will discuss in a later chapter (Halliday 1993). The first part is what he calls *language learning*, which generally maps how we learn our first language. The second is *learning through language*, which points out that language is the fundamental tool of nearly all other learning. Finally, *learning about language* turns our attention to how we all arrive at a point where the language itself can be an important object of study. To quote Halliday, "With this formulation I was trying to establish two unifying principles: that we should recognize not only a developmental continuity right through from birth to adult life, with language in home, neighborhood, primary school, secondary school, and place of work, but also a structural continuity running through all components and processes of learning" (113). Although some teachers and researchers might disagree, Halliday is suggesting that *learning language is learning itself.* ELD teachers who are able to negotiate this widened but complicated view of language have a privileged perspective.

Moreover, it is difficult—for me, anyway—to imagine an educator who is not compelled by language in all its complicated glory. Consider a child—almost any child, anywhere in the world, growing up in any culture. Placed in an environment where language is heard, that child, without any direct instruction, will learn the fundamentals of human speech by age three, and sometimes earlier. She will gain control of the sounds, the syntax, and the morphology of whatever language she hears with such ease that the process appears magical. But magic it is not. Our capacity for language acquisition is the product of a peculiar natural and cultural history thousands and thousands of years old, but one that is largely hidden from our modern understanding.

Nevertheless, the development of oral language has allowed our species to "own" the planet. For instance, human speech gave our ancestors the capacity to communicate across distances when hunting and to share thoughts while working (when hands are busy); very likely, language is the engine that has driven advances in human cognition. The biologist Edward O. Wilson (1998) wrote that

> the human attainment of high intelligence and culture ranks as the last of the four great steps in the overall history of life. They followed one upon the other at roughly one-billion-year intervals. The first was the beginning of life itself, in the form of simple bacterium-like organisms. Then came the origin of the complex eukaryotic cell through the assembly of the nucleus and other membrane-enclosed organelles into a tightly organized unit. With the eukaryotic building block available, the next advance was the origin of large, multi-cellular animals such as crustaceans and mollusks, whose movements were guided by sense organs and central nervous systems. Finally, to the grief of most preexisting life forms, came humanity. (107)

To my mind, language has been the engine that has led us to "high intelligence." The degree to which we can use that intelligence to alter what looks to be a rocky future for the planet will depend largely on our ability to understand and sympathize with others, which, in turn, de-

Language has been the engine that has led us to "high intelligence."

pends on understanding one another through language. As ELD teachers, we are easily convinced that we are working, for better or worse, to create a larger human community.

Geopolitics

Human disruptions on a global scale often work in favor of the ELD teacher. No one prefers it this way, but it is an inescapable truth. For instance, civil war in Somalia, combined with a rare loosening in U.S. immigration policy, resulted in thousands of refugees making their way to the United States. Complicated settlement agreements meant more work for ELD teachers in St. Paul, Minnesota, and the other midwestern cities where many Somali refugees were offered a place to live. Another example entails the millions of Vietnamese refugees seeking resettlement in the United States, many of whom endured hardships beyond imagination escaping their nation after the fall of Saigon in 1974. This massive immigration resulted in work for ELD teachers in places such as Garden Grove and San Jose, California; Houston, Texas; and New Orleans, Louisiana, all cities where over 1 million Vietnamese families were placed between 1974 and the early 1990s. Although immigration from Vietnam has slowed, reverberations from the Vietnam War remain.

Of course, no thoughtful person would favor these events, but without these upheavals, a great many ELD teachers in the United States would not have had the chance to practice their profession, nor would they have the opportunity to help prepare their colleagues for such work. Immigration does sometimes occur as a consequence of positive events (e.g., an engineer or physician from China receives a U.S. work permit), but for noticeable growth in ELL populations there is no substitute for disasters.

Unfortunately, geopolitical events are stubbornly unpredictable, making it difficult for ELD teachers to know which language to study next. Consider a more recent example: it remains to be seen whether U.S. policy will change with respect to the many thousands, perhaps millions, of Iraqis who wish to immigrate to the United States as a consequence of the war with Iraq. Although we cannot know for certain the number, many Iraqis were covert enemies of Saddam Hussein's regime, and many have willingly assisted the U.S. war effort—and yet the United States by 2007 had issued only fifty special visas to Iraqi translators and other diplomats (Swarns 2007). We might expect that a truly international resolution to the Iraq War will see the United States and other Western nations accepting Iraqi refugees. In the meantime, Syria has been the primary destination for many middle-class Iraqis, but their children are not allowed to attend Syrian schools. Sweden, alone among the Western nations, has allowed for more than 20,000 Iraqi refugees. The children among them are now learning Swedish and English in the public schools.

Recent immigration patterns in Europe also underscore the intersection of geopolitics and ELD teaching. A declining birthrate combined with a growing economy in many European countries has meant a great migration of low-skilled workers from the Maghreb, primarily the countries of Morocco, Algeria, and Tunisia, resulting in schools filled with children who speak a dialect of Arabic and want to learn French, English, or German.

GEOPOLITICS IN THE UNITED STATES AND MEXICO. As compelling as these stories are, the most enduring geopolitical predicament affecting ELD teachers in the United States is the result of the ongoing need for cheap labor in the United States coupled with a stubbornly high unemployment rate in rural Mexico (as high as 50 percent in some areas). These two factors have encouraged tens of millions of people to emigrate from Mexico to the United States, with or without documentation. This story is worth exploring in some depth because it is the one that has had the greatest effect on ELD teachers in this country.

Even though we could begin our analysis much earlier, I will start in the early 1980s, when Mexico experienced an economic crisis that forced it to adopt several fundamental economic reforms (Cragg and Epelbaum 1996). Partly as a consequence of the North American Free Trade Agreement, the Mexican government turned toward a more market-driven economy. It encouraged expansive trade and foreign investment, privatized many state-owned enterprises, reformed the tax structure, and deregulated many industries. Soon employment and wages increased dramatically for the urban middle class in Mexico, resulting in a dramatic increase in wage inequality for those in rural regions. Workers with postsecondary education and more experience saw their wages rise while less-skilled workers in rural Mexico were largely left behind. In other words, the rich got richer and the poor got poorer. Combine this condition with an increasing need for cheap labor in the United States during rapid economic expansion in the U.S. economy during the 1990s, and the result is easy to predict.

The Center for Immigration Studies (CIS) puts the number of undocumented workers and their family members at about 11 million in 2007. (Though the CIS is staunchly anti-immigrant, their data appear to be accurate.) The vast majority of undocumented workers emigrate from the rural regions of Mexico, most notably

Undocumented is the nonpejorative term: the term illegal can only be invoked when one provides a false work permit or Social Security number. I am willing to use the term illegal worker but only if we apply the same term to the businesses that employ undocumented workers (illegal employers). The children of undocumented workers are not "illegal" because they are not working.

the states of Oaxaca, Michoacán, and Jalisco. Many of them begin their working lives in the United States in agriculture, a historical starting point.

An example from the Watsonville, California, area provides but one story of the relationship between Mexican labor and agribusiness, and how teachers who have an interest in geopolitics are suited for ELD teaching. California's central coast is cool and moist. It rarely freezes within three miles of the ocean; in fact, the temperature seems stuck at about 65 degrees Fahrenheit. Hot, sunny, 100-degree days only 25 miles inland bring cooling fog to the coast. Combining the mild weather with a vast irrigation system, the region is perfectly suited for growing strawberries, which are now one of the most lucrative crops in the United States. Advances in growing technology, as well as better distribution, have made the strawberry a common delicacy across the nation and even the world (Wells 1996). At the same time, growing and harvesting strawberries is very labor intensive. In spite of many attempts to mechanize harvesting, the human hand remains the only tool adequate to the task of picking the delicate, almost skinless, ripe strawberry. And the work is very hard. Bending over for seven to eight hours a day strains the back, and repeated muscle movements cause an unnatural fatigue. Further, the picking of each strawberry requires a subtle action, balanced between the "give" of the stalk and the softness of the strawberry itself. It would be much easier to just yank, but the fruit is fragile and easily bruised. As a consequence of these challenging working conditions, strawberry growers have trouble finding enough "legal" workers in the United States and therefore hire workers from Mexico, who may or may not have the proper work documentation.

False documents are easy to obtain. Rings of counterfeiters produce bogus Social Security cards and work permits. Furthermore, as a result of the "amnesty" law of 1986, employers are not required to verify the authenticity of work documents. Thus we find once again that the

U.S. economy will find low-wage workers when it needs them.

If we apply our knowledge of the strawberry industry, what might we predict given current economic conditions in the United States and Mexico? Pia Orrenius and Madeline Zavodny (2005) demonstrate the complexity of the issue, pointing out that a rise in incomes in Mexico would enable *more* workers and their families to bear the cost of illegally entering the United States. So, would an improvement in Mexico's economy reduce immigration? These writers suggest that an increase in wages among Mexican workers might not reduce undocumented immigration, but rather cause a shift in those who can *afford* to immigrate.

Focus point

Teachers who take an interest in learning about the relationship between geopolitics and immigration, and local tensions such as the strawberry agribusiness example, are well suited for ELD instruction because they not only will have a grasp of what the future might hold for their work but will also know more of the lives of their students.

Porfirio Díaz, former president of Mexico (b. 1830, d. 1915), was a ruthless politician. He rigged elections and even hired assassins to kill his opponents, but even he recognized Mexico's predicament. In a famous statement, he shares his view: "¡Pobre México! ¡Tan lejos de Dios y tan cerca de los Estados Unidos!" (Poor Mexico, so far from God and so close to the United States!)

Democracy

**Cross-Reference
For a sustained
discussion of
democracy and
education, see
Book 5,
Chapter 5.**

I believe that the public schools and their role in preparing immigrant (i.e., ELL) students are linked to the great democratic ideal, a vision of a society yet unrealized. The great democracy exists in a place where each and every person is given a chance to challenge existing social limits, where each and every person is fitted equitably with the tools for that challenge, and where we encourage everyone to give it a try.

John Dewey wrote, "Education is a regulation of the process of coming to share in the social consciousness" (Dewey 1897, 80). Dewey's use of the term *social consciousness* might be a proxy for *democracy,* and *regulation* might be considered a term akin to *access.* For many, many reasons, contemporary schools do not fit us equitably with the tools for challenging these social limits; we must therefore resolve to work harder to achieve this democratic ideal.

Public schools and their role in preparing immigrant students are linked to the great democratic ideal.

ELD teachers are troubled by the fact that their students and families face challenges to joining in democracy, sharing in social consciousness, and their role in the regulation of the process. Consider that a great many parents of ELLs, as immigrants, legal or otherwise, cannot vote (a topic we will address at length in the final chapter). This is a striking contrast to just what is facing ELD teachers who see the democratic ideal as part of their work. Without even the minimal right to cast a ballot, what chance do ELLs and their families have in shaping the course of the community or nation?

How do ELD teachers assist families in coming to share in the social consciousness when lacking the opportunity to vote is accompanied by racism and **linguicism**? (Linguicism is a form of prejudice, an "-ism" along the lines of racism, ageism, or sexism. Broadly defined, it involves an individual making judgments about another's wealth, education, social status, character, and/or other traits based on choice and use of language.)

Key concept
linguicism

Think for a moment: What are some of the specific challenges social studies teachers might have when teaching children of undocumented workers? How might those challenges be addressed?

As a nation of immigrants, we are quick to tell our own version of the family immigration tale and its hardships. Many Americans can tell how their ancestors arrived in the United States with little or no money, speaking no English, and by hard work and perseverance came to be full participants in the nation's political, economic, and educational life. As ELD teachers, we must reconsider these tales for what they are and update them for our time. We first must recognize that immigrants to the United States have never been uniformly treated; based on their country of origin, some were welcomed, others not (Flores 2003; King 2000). Even if past immigrant experiences had been equivalent, why do we think excessive hardship and a slow and painful march to democratic participation are good? ELD teachers can help their students grow in their affiliation with a new nation while maintaining ties to their families' history, but finding such a balance is challenging work, especially when U.S. political leaders have been so unequivocal on the issue of immigration.

IMMIGRATION REFORM AND REACTIONARY POLITICS. Working on this book coincided with the final months of the George W. Bush administration, a time to reconsider the failed initiatives of one of the least popular presidents in U.S. history. For example, Bush had a chance to unite both political parties and leave a lasting reform with his suggested immigration policy. The proposal was modest by most standards. It established a guest worker program and would have allowed those in the United States without documentation a chance to gain legal status by paying a series of fees and filing multiple documents, while also adding more border controls. Supported by leading Democrats and most moderate Republicans, Bush lost the support of the right wing of his own party, and the bill died. Senate leaders had no intention of bringing it back until after Bush left office.

Worse than the defeat of the Immigration Bill, which was cautiously supported by immigration advocates, was the development of an opposition bill sponsored by Rep. James Sensenbrenner (R-WI) and thirty-five other House members. Known as the Border Protection, Antiterrorism, and Illegal Immigration Control Act of 2005, the bill revised the definition of "aggravated felony" to include all smuggling offenses and illegal entry and reentry crimes. If the defeat of the Immigration Bill represented a lost chance to help 11 million people grow closer to full democratic participation, Sensenbrenner's bill was quite the opposite: a direct attack on the immigrant community. So it was no surprise when millions of undocumented immigrants protested in the only way they could: by marching. On May 1, 2006, millions of people walked instead of going to work. Some protesters called the marches "a day without an immigrant" to emphasize the importance of the labor provided by undocumented workers (Pulido 2007).

As I had heard of the May 1 marches beforehand, I planned to participate, but instead I spent the day in the classroom of a friend and former student who taught social studies in a high school nearby. The school, which is 90 percent Latino—of which many students are first-generation immigrants and ELLs—had already experienced at least two disrupted days when students skipped school in protest of the bill. For its part, the school had been trying very hard to discourage students from missing school. Teachers and administrators tried to impress upon the students that they would not be excused for their absence and tests or other important activities would not be rescheduled. They also knew that for every student who marched instead of coming to school, the school district would lose about $50. In a state such as California, which funds public education so poorly, this was revenue the district could not afford to lose. They also argued that missing school was counterproductive to the larger cause of opposing the legislation.

My day in the social studies classes, which included a few periods of ELLs, was all I had hoped for. Students were eager to share the reasons they came to school and also the reasons some of their peers did not. They generally reported that most of the absent students were not particularly invested in the cause but rather used it as an excuse to miss school. I later found this to be more or less true. One white girl said that she was called a racist on the way to school because she was not marching. A former ELL student told us that his parents had closed their store and were marching, but that they had made him go to school. *Learn,* they had told him; that is how you can protest. We all thought that both stories were valuable lessons for democracy, and my teacher friend made a point of using all the students' comments in a future lesson on civic participation. As an ELD teacher, she could hardly afford not to make curricula out of the historical event.

Focus point

It is difficult to overstate the dilemmas facing immigrant ELLs and their families. Hoping to gain full participation in U.S. life but with ties to home nations, they tread lightly upon the political landscape. On a recent Univision news program, I saw a familiar story about extended families separated by two countries. The international border on the beach between U.S. California and Mexico's Baja California, where massive steel walls have been constructed to separate the two countries, has become a popular site for families to visit and have picnics. Fortuitously, the walls are no match for the pounding sea, and chain-link fencing has been used to fill in the spaces where the steel planks have separated. Through the fence, news footage showed a child's hand reaching for his grandmother, the two separated by a single, small fence but two enormous nations. I do not know this child's teacher, but I am almost certain he is learning English from her. I am also certain he has lots of questions about his predicament. How will she answer?

Culture

The sociologist Louis Wirth once said that the proper definition of *culture* is "everything that we take for granted." Imagine this definition applied to the schools we attended or now teach in. We have in mind a fixed view of the culture of a school primarily because we simply assume that it must look the way it does. We take for granted the fact that children must read certain kinds of texts, do mathematical problems, listen to teachers, and obey certain rules. Schools have a specialized culture that has been shaped by forces so powerful and historical we have no idea where they came from, but we nevertheless abide by them. As an example of a cultural practice whose origin is now largely unknown, some individuals wear a wedding ring on the third finger of their left hand. Most of us have no idea that in classical times, it was believed that the third finger on the left hand was the location of the vein of love, and therefore a direct connection to the heart. Today, we simply take it for granted.

One of the more recent challenges in the study of culture in schools—and one that appears to be long lasting—is the relationship between the culture of the teacher and the culture of the students. For many years, this relationship was of little concern to anyone. It was simply assumed that teachers, as representatives of the dominant culture, would impart their cultural values and beliefs to the students, irrespective of how those beliefs may conflict with those of the students. We have, with good reason, come to question our earlier neglect of this relationship, asking perhaps if the cultural mismatch between the teacher and the students could prevent ELL students from achieving to their highest capabilities.

The books, materials, physical spaces, and social demographics of teachers offer only an indication of what a culture values and believes. These artifacts alone are just a portent of the full expression of culture in a school. When we add students, teachers, administrators, and parents, the culture presents itself, with all its triumphs and foibles, almost by magic. The interaction of all these features makes the study of culture in schools complex.

Therefore, what we gain by seeing the depth and breadth of a culture in the school is balanced by the prospect of a much more complicated cultural admixture.

Focus point

Successful ELD teachers are likely to recognize clearly the "taken-for-granteds" in the school because they so often exist in sharp contrast to the culture of their students. Nothing points out the arbitrary nature of school culture more than when we must explain it all to someone who has never seen it before. However, there is not necessarily something wrong about the culture of the school. Raising your hand to speak, an obvious part of school culture, can be stifling, but if we want to hear our students' views, they cannot all speak at once. Some have argued that teaching ELLs is centrally about learning the culture of the students. I agree that knowing the culture of the students is crucial, but if we leave it there, we have come less than halfway. ELD teachers must understand not only the cultures of their students but also how they will merge or accommodate the cultures of the students *and* the culture of the school.

Think for a moment: What are some school-related cultural practices that visitors or students from other countries might not be aware of?

GAINING PERSPECTIVE ON CULTURE AND LEARNING. I think that most ELD teachers who have given the topic considerable thought would say that merging the cultures of students with the school is very complicated. Schools have the task of transmitting the terms of a society, often reflecting the culture in which they live, even altering it, all while working within it. To this already complex and dense cultural mixture, add our own peculiar expectations for U.S. schools, which include fitting students with tools to change their culture (moving out of a culture of poverty, for instance), and the task is further complicated. This condition reminds me of Otto Neurath's point that studying language is like disassembling and reassembling a boat while it remains in the water. We are surrounded, even immersed, by the object of our study. We cannot examine language without using it, just as we cannot forsake our own culture before we study it. Because we all experience schooling, we have no external point of reference: no land, no pier from which to gain perspective. I would argue that the task of teaching ELLs is made more complex because, following Neurath, we are not simply trying to build any boat, we are trying to build a very fast and sturdy boat.

Think for a moment: What is the difference between language and culture? Are they always distinct?

Second-language researchers have been explicit about the importance of culture in L2 teaching and have shaped theories of cultural adjustment to their own purposes. One of the more enduring and, I would argue, compelling theories of culture and language learning comes from the work of John Schumann (Schumann 1976, 1990). Schumann draws on the concept of social distance to describe the metaphorical route that L2 learners must take from their home culture to that of the target culture. His theories have generally been successfully applied to adult learners who have immigrated from one distinct culture to another, and his general theory works for younger ELLs and their families. At the heart of his theory is the linguistic concept of pidginization. Our common understanding of pidgin is that it is a low-status language, but this view is not altogether correct, and in order to understand Schumann's theory we must explore it further.

PIDGINS AND CREOLES AS LANGUAGE FORMS. A pidgin is, in fact, an individual speaker's attempt to meld

Key concept
pidgin

a native and the target language, and what emerges is a combination of the two. **Pidgins** are more formally described as "a contact vernacular among people who need to communicate but do not share a common language" (Siegel 1997, 86). If many people are put in the same linguistic and social position, their pidgins are likely to have similar features. The most commonly known examples of pidgins have been those forged from the need for slaves to communicate with their often brutal masters. But, there are less violent examples of pidgins, such as the pidgin formed when modern people must communicate in commercial settings. In Schumann's theory of social distance, L2 learners living in a new culture as they learn a second language become cultural "pidgins," achieving a transitional balance between their native culture and the new one. However, following the strict definition of pidgin, speakers move past these transitional phases and either adopt one language or the other, or, as in the case of the French Haitian language, the pidgin becomes widely used. By borrowing lexical elements of both languages but forming its own grammatical rules, it can become a language in itself. In this case, the pidgin has thus become what is known as creole language. A creole, then, is a pidgin that becomes a community's native language. Creoles are languages in their own right that are learned by successive generations.

Returning to Schumann's metaphor, learners of a new culture typically achieve a cultural balance somewhat akin to a linguistic creole, a fusion of cultural values and practices that are then passed on to children. It is possible for an L2 learner to remain pidginized in a cultural midpoint, but this place is uncomfortable. Neither assimilating to the new culture nor adapting or accommodating to a blended one, such learners are caught between cultures, not quite fitting into either. For such learners, the "distance" between the two cultures, or at least their capacity for negotiating it, is too far.

Schumann's theory has been critiqued for equating culture and language without noting the important differences between them. Cultures give rise to languages, not the other way around. Further, we know that teaching language is sometimes considered a proxy for cultural learning, but as Gail Robinson-Stuart and Honorine Nocon (1996) point out, there is no "magic carpet ride" that takes students from understanding the language to understanding the culture.

My own research suggests that Latino youth gang members provide a good example of individuals who have been forced to live midway between one culture and another (Téllez and Estep 1997). As immigrants or the children of immigrants, youth who are attracted to gang life often begin school as ELLs, but the distance between their native Spanish and English, as well as the distance between their home culture—most often rooted in rural Mexico—and contemporary U.S. society, is far. Consequently, they develop a pidgin cultural frame. As the national expert on Latino youth gangs, my colleague James Diego Vigil, suggests, "for a small but considerable portion of barrio (neighborhood) youth with problematic backgrounds, the street gang has arisen as a competitor of other institutions, such as family and schools, to guide and direct self-identification" (Vigil 1988b, 421). The gang acts as a cultural space between the home and the new culture and, in this instance in particular, becomes an unhealthy alternative. Vigil has related the "slang" of Latino youth gangs to the cultural space they inhabit (Vigil 1988a). In a similar linguistic adaptation, Latino youth gangs develop a pidgin that turns English words to new purposes and invents entirely new terms (e.g., neither Spanish nor English, *ruca* means "girlfriend" or "good friend who is a girl").

When I have shared this work with ELD teachers, their natural inclination is to wonder how to help such youth negotiate the two cultural worlds and prevent them from falling into gang life. I tell them honestly that I am not certain the schools can influence that decision. Without the capability to intervene more widely in the community and family resources, schools are limited in their ability to help these youth. In fact, in some communities we might argue that some gang members are not caught in a pidgin culture but rather a creole one. That is, it is not rare to find two or three generations of gang members in some communities. What I can tell teachers is that knowing the culture of their ELLs is vital if they hope to help their students progress to full participation in U.S. society. But teachers rarely come from the same cultural backgrounds as their ELLs.

Focus point

ELD teachers do not mind being perpetually on the lookout for moments when an expression of student home culture is manifested. They do not mind taking on the learning of a second or third culture. They recognize that this learning cannot be like the detached form of the anthropologist, but rather of a teacher, who plays a central role in the lives of his or her students.

CONCLUSION

Teaching ELLs requires knowledge beyond what others teachers must know. In my view, ELD teachers must hold a deep and abiding knowledge of language and languages, a commitment to understanding the geopolitical events that influence their students (and future students) and their families, a desire to understand their students' cultures in ways that make them more able to connect home culture to school culture, and last, a devotion to the democratic ideals that have served to create opportunities for immigrants around the world while recognizing that democracy is an ideal, a yet incomplete form of human organization.

Teaching has been unfairly characterized as a normalized profession; some have even called it domesticated. By this I mean that teachers are not widely associated with the broad, worldly issues that confront us all and that fascinate many. Teachers, we are told, are not intellectuals. I have tried in this chapter to roundly dispel that myth and argue that ELD teaching is suited for those whose reach is far, and whose grasp is equal to it.

DISCUSSION QUESTIONS

1. Think about the geopolitics that may have affected your region in the last six to twelve months. This could include new legislation, world disasters, or even new energy policies. How are these events likely to have an effect on the children who attend your school (a) next fall, and (b) five years from now? How can you prepare for it?

2. What other languages would you like to learn or continue learning at this time? Teachers are notorious for being resourceful, especially with budget and time constraints. List some resources that will help you to achieve your language goals.

3. Most researchers would agree that you cannot learn about cultures in a textbook, but perhaps in a book of native art, poetry, or literature. What are other sources of learning about other peoples' cultures that you have access to?

4. Consider: How can you, as a teacher, support your students of other cultures in the prevention of entering into gang activity? What do you need to know about their cultures, and how can you find out?

FURTHER READING

Halliday, M. A. K. 1975. *Learning How to Mean—Explorations in the Development of Language.* London: Edward Arnold.
   This book introduces readers to the development of our linguistic system. Halliday studies his own son's language development and finds some surprising features of early meaning making.

Landes, Ruth. 1965. *Culture in American Education*. New York: Wiley and
    Sons.
    This landmark book documents how teachers in eastern Los Angeles
    County learned about their Mexican American students' lives and then
    acted on that knowledge in their classrooms.
Sanchez, George. 1993. *Becoming Mexican American: Ethnicity, Culture, and
    Identity in Chicano Los Angeles, 1900–1945*. New York: Oxford University
    Press.
    Sanchez provides a history of immigrants in Los Angeles and documents
    the creative ways that families have thrived in spite of extreme poverty and
    discrimination.

CHAPTER TWO

ENGLISH-LANGUAGE LEARNERS IN THE UNITED STATES

A Statistical and Biographical Portrait

- What's Important About the Statistics?
- Who Are Our ELLs?
- Mexican Americans: A Portrait for Our Times
- The Immigrant "Threat"
- Can a Second Culture Be "Learned"?
- Cultural Knowledge and the Curriculum of the Sacred

T EACHERS MUST BE AWARE of what their students already know before they can teach them anything new. A banal statement, right? What thoughtful modern educator does not believe this? Although I am certain that most teachers take this view for granted, I wonder how many have thought deeply enough about it for the statement to have any real meaning or impact on their instruction. As an ELD teacher you must, of course, know your students, but such an understanding is likely to be more challenging because ELLs almost always represent a culture and therefore a body of previous knowledge that differs from your own. *The work of the ELD teacher is to learn about his or her students in a way that does not stereotype them but also draws some direct conclusions regarding how teachers should connect the content of school to what students already know.* To accomplish this task, I want to share with you some statistical data and later some foundational understandings of two cultural groups. I believe that this twofold analysis

Focus point

will provide you with some specific ideas that can help you to teach ELLs more effectively.

WHAT'S IMPORTANT ABOUT THE STATISTICS?

There are several reasons to know numerical data on ELLs. First, ELD teachers are often the ambassadors for ELLs in the wider society, and if they cannot be succinct and accurate about who ELLs are, then the rest of the nation has little chance of understanding our immigrant communities. Family or neighborhood gatherings routinely offer ELD teachers the chance to dispel myths about immigrant students and their families, so you must know the data well.

More times than I care to mention, I have had to explain to noneducators why the term *illegal immigrant* is not accurate. I have also had to point out the real reasons why so many Mexican citizens would risk their lives to immigrate to the United States.

Second, ELD teachers must be able to anticipate trends regarding their student population, and an examination of recent data will help to prepare educators for what is to come. Although numbers never reflect the experiences of individual students and their families, an understanding of ELLs from a wider perspective can be used in concert with more local knowledge to create a coherent educational plan.

Third, ELLs themselves should have a broader view of immigrant families and language learners. Thus, ELD teachers can use the following data in various ways to help their students understand their own communities

Think for a moment: What stereotypes or assumptions about ELL students have people expressed to you, as a teacher, outside of the classroom? Do you think you were successful in representing ELLs in a more accurate way?

more fully. For instance, I know that few secondary Latino students in the United States understand the political force they will become. Secondary ELL students in particular should know the demographic trends. One of the best social studies lessons I have seen invited ELLs to explore the census figures, trying to figure out what the U.S. population might look like in fifty years. When the class of largely Latino students realized that their communities were growing and might soon be a majority in many states, they felt empowered, but they also understood that their communities would grow in their responsibilities.

Finally, recognizing students as members of a unique cultural group, a topic addressed later in this chapter, is now accepted as crucial knowledge for teachers. To paraphrase a well-known writer in the area of "culturally relevant pedagogy," teachers must respect and use the reality, history, and perspectives of students as an integral part of educational practice. There is no counterposition to this statement, but what does it mean practically? Few writers in this area are willing to be specific about what such platitudes mean for teaching. Furthermore, I find most "multiculturalists" unwilling to make any generalizations regarding cultural groups, but without having some general ideas about what particular groups value, how can we alter practice? In this chapter I will attempt to both draw generalizations and make specific suggestions. Knowing how to link or use student culture in the classroom cannot be routinized or even predicted, but learning about student culture can, at the very least, make teaching less humiliating for students whose culture does not match that of the teachers.

Think for a moment: What are ways to effectively validate and recognize other cultures in the classroom without stereotyping or essentializing a culture?

Perhaps our species' most common and disastrous mistake is the belief that human cultures are "things," immutable and somehow floating above the very people who create them. Cultural anthropologists and others call this error *reification*, noting that when we turn a dynamic process into an imagined concrete object, we make a complex process easier to reckon. In one particularly interesting study, Gerd Baumann (1996) documented how nonimmigrant groups living in West London viewed culture in a way that "seemed at once to reify their own cultures and communities, and to deny their own reifications." Reification seems to allow us the capacity to think of cultures as static objects while failing to recognize we are objectifying them in the first place. It also appears that we are most capable of reifying cultures that are not our own.

Human cultures are constantly changing, and to consider them as an unalterable object is to miss the essence of culture itself. Like all living things, cultures must change—we might use the term *grow*—or they die. Not only do all cultures change, but there is no reliable way to benchmark when a culture is moving "fast" or whether that movement is in a "good" or "bad" direction. It is a common fallacy that modern industrialized cultures are changing more rapidly than those with less outward technology.

WHO ARE OUR ELLS?

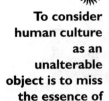

To consider human culture as an unalterable object is to miss the essence of culture itself.

One data point on which I think all U.S. educators can agree is that the number of ELLs, especially in some regions, is substantial and growing. If we begin with the broadest data collected by the U.S. Census, we find that over 6.5 million children and youth ages 5–17 speak a language other than English at home; native Spanish speakers account for 4.7 million of this total (U.S. Department of Commerce and U.S. Census Bureau 2000). However, not all these students are ELLs. A great many

Think for a moment: How are English learners in school today the same as or different from the early European immigrants to the United States, who also spoke a language other than English? Have the needs of these children changed?

of them speak a language other than English at home but are either bilingual, and thus may never have been considered an ELL, or learned English at school and are thus no longer considered an ELL. Data show that 5.1 million children enrolled in U.S. schools are ELLs (Pearson 2006), a figure that represents approximately 10.5 percent of all students. Approximately 80 percent of all ELLs are native Spanish speakers (Loeffler 2005). The remaining ELLs speak one of the 450 world languages found in U.S. schools.

After Spanish, however, the languages represented are more evenly divided. For instance, Vietnamese, the second most represented language behind Spanish, with approximately 89,000 ELLs, accounts for just under 2 percent of the total ELL population. Hmong is third, with about 1.5 percent, followed by Chinese (Cantonese) and Korean, each about 1 percent of the total. The remaining languages (e.g., Arabic, Armenian, Chuukese, French, Haitian Creole, Hindi, Japanese, Khmer, Lao, Mandarin, Marshallese, Navajo, Polish, Portuguese, Punjabi, Russian, Serbo-Croatian, Tagalog, Urdu, and others) spoken by ELLs in U.S. schools represent about 14 percent of all ELLs.

These national figures do not, however, reveal the concentrations of ELLs in certain parts of the country. California's ELL population is 1.6 million—about a third of the national total and equaling one-fourth of all students enrolled in public schools in the state (California Legislative Analyst's Office 2007). Over 85 percent of these students speak Spanish as their native language, and an equal percentage are economically disadvantaged.

Think for a moment: What features of the six states listed below may have led them to being the host of the majority of the ELL population in the United States?

Across the United States, over 61 percent of all ELLs attend school in one of six states, listed here in rank order: California, Texas, Florida, New York, Illinois, and Arizona (Capps et al. 2005).

The most populous ELL state figures do not, however, reveal another set of data showing the threefold (or more) increase in the ELL populations of certain other states. For instance, in 1995, South Carolina's public schools enrolled approximately 2,000 ELLs. Ten years later, in 2005, there were nearly 16,000. The trend is also seen in a host of other states, mostly those in the South. Kentucky saw a 417 percent increase over the same ten-year period. North Carolina's growth was 370 percent, and the state now enrolls over 70,000 ELLs.

Cultural Facts and Artifacts, Reality and Perception

One consequence of our national interest in race and ethnicity has meant that schools and government agencies have been much more likely to keep track of students' races or ethnicities than their language status, although as you can see by the data just reported, this bias is slowly changing. Nevertheless, in order to better understand ELLs, both statistically and biographically, ELD teachers must explore the cultures of their ELLs, which may or may not be tied to a national or racial identity. No single book could possibly perform the task of detailing each of the cultures represented by all ELL language groups in the United States (there are over 450!), so I will focus on two. As the data demonstrate, Latinos, specifically those of Mexican descent, represent the largest subgroup of ELLs in the United States. It therefore makes sense to explore the cultural background of these students. I have also chosen to study those ELLs whose native language is Vietnamese. These portrayals were not chosen at random, although it is true that they represent a greater percentage of ELLs than many other language groups. I admit that these are the cultural groups most familiar to me.

Culture gives rise to language, not the other way around.

Thinking About the Connection Between Language and Culture

As we move from thinking about students who speak a language other than English to considering them as students who represent a culture, it is important to remember that culture gives rise to language, not the other way around. Human languages are varied, that is clear enough, and as important as they might seem to maintaining culture, a language or dialect is a tool of the culture rather than a direct representation of it. Unfortunately, some of the common mythology surrounding language and culture has encouraged the incorrect view that language shapes culture. Informally, this view has been called the "Eskimo" myth, which suggests that Inuit speakers have many more words for snow than English speakers and thus the evidence that our "reality" is shaped by language. Once the myth became commonplace, linguists and anthropologists alike (e.g., Pullum 1991) made efforts to discredit it. Although a full exploration of the myth would take too much time, the simple way to expose it is to think of English adjectives and nouns as capable of forming a single word, which is a common feature of many languages, including Inuit. If we merge wet and snow to make "wetsnow" we now have a single word. Now think of all the English "words" for snow we can make (e.g., "packedsnow," "icysnow," "springsnow"). Therefore, because the Inuit have multiple words for snow does not provide evidence of their cultural reality. It is more a consequence of the rules of their language. The formal proposition of this myth has been called the "Sapir-Whorf" hypothesis, now shown to be both widely misunderstood and incorrect (Berthoff 1988).

I want to underscore the relationship between language and culture because I have found that educators (including myself at times) have a tendency to ignore ELLs as cultural beings and instead conceive of them as only students needing to learn English. But moving from data that describe a student's language background to those that describe her ethnicity changes the way she is perceived. We are conditioned to respond to numbers as though they were dispassionate facts. But when numbers reflect the characteristics of actual people and their differences beyond just their native language, they lose their imagined objectivity. In particular, data about ethnicity, as in a census, are as likely to elicit great interest, even passion. Consequently, before presenting the census data regarding the statistical portrait of ELLs, it is important to recognize how numbers can be used for more than simple representation. ELD teachers, in turn, must recognize that while their primary interest is in understanding students who are nonnative speakers of English, such students almost always bring with them a culture that, by definition, is "nondominant."

MEXICAN AMERICANS: A PORTRAIT FOR OUR TIMES

The growth of the Latino population—in particular, Mexican Americans—has come as news to many, and the U.S. Census of 2000 made this point clear. In fact, the reaction to the release of the 2000 census was shrill, essentially summarized as "The Latinos Are Coming! We've Got to Do Something!" The national press seemed to report the latest figures as a warning, an attempt to scare the country into reacting to the "runaway" growth among Latinos. A recent U.S. Census report shows that the total number of children under age five who are Latino and of Mexican descent rose from about 19 percent in 2000 to

This road sign on Interstate 5 near the U.S.-Mexico border in California cautions drivers to watch for undocumented families crossing the freeway. Who would risk their life to enter the United States unless they had no other option? (courtesy of Roger J. Wendell)

24 percent in 2007. Perhaps the stories were meant to spur increased surveillance on the U.S.-Mexico border, a desire that has partially materialized. After the terrorist attacks of September 11, 2001, policymakers and analysts who wanted more resources for border security between the United States and Mexico used the attacks to bolster their argument, even though the hijackers came through the U.S.-Canadian, not Mexican, border.

I argue that the reporting of this type of data encourages a kind of reification. When data are shown only for very recent changes and projected trends, they tend to suggest that the ethnic balance at the present time emerged out of nowhere, making the complex cultural influences behind such numbers a "thing." The U.S. ethnic composition is constantly changing, so to think that future growth by any ethnic group will significantly alter the U.S. culture defies logic. "Hispanics" were a fast-growing population in the 1950s and early 1960s, a so-called high watermark of U.S. culture. Past immigrant

Think for a moment: What kinds of geopolitical or economic forces might attract immigrants to a particular part of the nation or to a specific section of a city? Is there anything that could help school districts predict these trends?

families became part of U.S. culture; to be sure, they did not assimilate completely nor did they alter it dramatically, but that is the nature of culture itself: it is hard to notice the changes at all from the "inside."

ELD teachers must be aware of the forces at work that attempt to reify U.S. culture and overstate the "loss" of U.S. culture when data on the growth of Latino immigrants, and therefore ELLs, are presented. Martha Gimenez (1997) points out the dangers of media portrayals of this growth when she writes:

> The mass media and politicians exploit data about the youth, higher fertility, and growth rates of the "Hispanic" population in ways that, ultimately, intensify racist fears among those worried about low white fertility, increase the likelihood of conflict with blacks (who see their communities competing for scarce resources with an ever-growing "minority" group), and strengthen stereotypes about "Hispanic" cultural traits. (227)

A superb recent book by Leo Chavez (2008) traces the recent history of immigrants from Mexico. As the number of volunteers ready to patrol the U.S.-Mexico border increased, so did the hundreds of thousands of men, women, and children who have marched in support of immigrant rights. Like Gimenez, Chavez uses the media stories and recent experiences of immigrants to show how prejudices and stereotypes have been used to malign an entire immigrant population. Many policy analysts and politicians have nurtured the view that Latinos, particularly Mexicans, are an invading force bent on reconquering land once considered their own. Through a perceived refusal to learn English and an "out of control" birthrate, neither of which is an accurate portrayal, many say that Latinos are destroying the American way of life. Chavez questions these assumptions and offers facts to counter the myth that Latinos are a threat to the security and prosperity of our nation.

THE IMMIGRANT "THREAT"

We might wonder whom Chavez is opposing. The view that Latinos are a "threat" to U.S. society might have once had adherents, but surely the nation has moved beyond such fears. Chavez argues that the United States remains mired in such views and that we need look no further than Samuel Huntington, the Harvard professor whose odd mix of political science and amateur anthropology continues to gain audience (his books sell tens of thousands of copies). Huntington once advocated that world conflicts would no longer exist among nation-states but rather between and among world cultures, of which he offhandedly identified eight (i.e., Western, Latin American, Islamic, Sinic [Chinese], Hindu, Orthodox, Japanese, and African). Because Huntington views Western culture (including the United States) as one entity and Latin American as another, he argues that the "influx" of Mexican immigrants will supplant the "Western" culture that now exists in the United States. Huntington seems to have raised reification errors to an astonishing new level while conveniently avoiding the fact that so-called Western culture in the United States is well represented by the cultural influence of the Mexican Americans already here.

How could Huntington continue to publish such analyses and be so widely read? First, U.S. politics have always nourished a version of populism that focuses on U.S. workers and their needs. With advocates as widely represented as Pat Buchanan, whose anti-immigrant stances are well-known, to more left-leaning politicians who often court the labor vote, populists exploit the view that rich elites are in control, making lots of money at the expense of the common worker. Populists have often been successful by forging a policy that promotes both U.S. isolationism and native-born (union) workers' rights, both of which are at odds with immigrant workers, undocumented or otherwise. **Populism** is a discourse that aims to support and favor the general whole of the electorate rather than elite lobbyist influences. Populism may comprise an ideology urging social and political system changes and/or a rhetorical style deployed by members of political or social movements.

Key concept
populism

Second, the number of foreign-born people residing in the United States (37 million) has reached a proportion of the U.S. population (12.4 percent) not seen since the early twentieth century. Of the foreign-born residents in the United States, approximately one-third are

As a teacher, take a moment to make an honest assessment of your views on immigrants. Does the immigrant "boom" make you nervous? Does it feel as if the nation cannot adequately "assimilate" all the immigrants now arriving? Do you fear that the culture will change so radically that you and your family will not recognize it? These concerns are not necessarily those of reactionaries like Huntington, and I know many teachers who share such views privately. As teachers of ELLs, we need to hold open conversations about our concerns, but I find all too often this dialogue never sees light. Find a trusted colleague and talk about your own family's history of immigration, inviting questions of each other about how the nation was altered by your own ancestors' arrival. The goal, to my mind, is to arrive at the view that new immigrants are no different from previous groups. Of course they will alter life in the United States, but so did each and every immigrant in the nation's past.

naturalized citizens, one-third are legal permanent residents, and one-third are undocumented residents (Passel 2007). These figures frighten many U.S. residents, who fear the influence of immigrants will radically change long-standing cultural patterns.

Third, many immigrants to the United States, especially those without documentation, tend to be poorer than people born in the United States. Specific to our interests, data show that ELLs are more than twice as likely to live in poverty than their native English-speaking counterparts (approximately 70 percent vs. 30 percent). Poverty rates among immigrants ply fears that they will drain money from social services and education meant for U.S.-born children and youth. Social scientists have recently admitted that trying to account for the total "cost" of immigration has failed, noting that various researchers have used only those data designed to support their argument (Vernez and McCarthy 1996). For instance, if we only examine the short-term costs of immigration, the need for social services and education is greater for immigrants than for native-born, but calculating the long-term benefits is nearly impossible. At some point, immigrants begin to contribute positively to the national economy. If this fact were not true, the United States would have failed generations ago.

These factors, among many others, work against the ELD teacher trying to help his or her students and their families adjust to life in the United States. Although the view held by some native-born Americans that immigrants are out to "take over" U.S. culture is wholly unfounded, I am not hopeful that politicians, in particular, will anytime soon stop their anti-immigrant polemic. For better or worse, taking an anti-immigration stance is politically savvy: (1) politicians can align themselves with workers in the United States, whether or not they are pro-labor, claiming that immigrants are taking jobs from the native-born, and (2) they can alienate immigrants and suffer no practical consequences on election day, because the vast majority of recent immigrants, both documented and undocumented, cannot vote because they are not citizens. It is that simple.

Without ambitions of supplanting the existing culture, why do immigrants, especially undocumented ones, risk the dangerous journey to the United States? Surveys of U.S. immigrants from throughout the world cite work opportunities, educational advantages, and freedom from political oppression as the primary reasons for coming to the United States. Of these three, work is by far the most common reason, especially among immigrants from Mexico, whose children make up the majority of ELLs in the United States.

The story of work opportunities for Mexican immigrants can be neatly captured in the example of the rise in the demand for processed or "cut-up" meat products. In 1963, U.S. consumers commonly bought whole chickens and cut them up themselves; processed chicken products then amounted to only 15.2 percent of total U.S. consumer chicken shipments (Kandel and Parrado 2005). By 1997, the cut-up total of the chicken market had grown to 86.9 percent. Buying chicken parts, sometimes already packaged in individually sealed bags, saves consumers time and allows them to purchase only the cuts they want. Naturally, meatpackers sought to satisfy the demand for cut-up products, but meat packaging is dangerous and tedious work, making it unattractive for any U.S.-born worker with alternatives. Lacking a willing labor pool, employers turned to immigrants from Mexico, who were willing to do the work at a low wage.

Think for a moment: What jobs are now largely performed by immigrant workers? What might be the next labor market that will attract immigrant workers?

In fact, in 2000, over 80 percent of all meatpacking workers in the United States were foreign-born, up from 15 percent just thirty years ago.

A Biographical Portrait of Two ELL Cultural Groups and Applications to Classroom Practice

Moving beyond a statistical portrait of ELLs might suggest that we begin by creating a list of common beliefs held and behaviors shown by a native language group in order to better understand our students. Although it is true that our human cognitive system is very good at categorizing when we find common attributes, applying this skill to a set of people is never warranted and our inclinations in this direction must be fought back continuously. One clearly wrong way to view a cultural group is through the lens of a stereotype. Developed from minimal observation and often by people who are not members of the described group, stereotypes are uncritically applied to individuals and very often lead to prejudice. Another method for categorizing a group of people borrows from the "scientific" work of scholars who study social groups. These descriptions are not stereotypes in the strict definition of the term because they are based on wide observations that make use of the tools of social scientists (systematic interviews or observations, for instance). But regardless of their purported scientific value, we will shortly see that generalizations cannot do much work in our efforts to learn or acquire culture. On the other hand, it is not uncommon for educators to speak of addressing the pedagogical needs of "diverse" students, rather than, for example, Mexican American, Korean American, or Hmong American students, although these three cultural groups' backgrounds and educational needs can be quite different (e.g., Téllez 2004). Finding a balance between meeting the needs of a particular language or social group without engaging in stereotypes or generalizations is our challenge.

The Cultural and Linguistic Background of Mexican American and Mexican-Descent Students

As we consider Mexican American students as cultural beings rather than just students who need to learn English, I would like to share the following list of supposed cultural features of Latinos.

In an article designed to help psychologists understand their Latino clients, Lorraine Gutierrez, Anna Yeakley, and Robert Ortega (2000) suggest that Latinos lean toward the following traits or dispositions: (1) a sense of identity and commitment to collectives and groups, rather than to the individual; (2) a focus on intergroup and intragroup harmony, with an avoidance of conflict and confrontation; (3) a loyalty and attachment to one's nuclear and extended family; (4) a preference for closeness in interpersonal space; (5) a flexible time orientation, with an emphasis on the "here and now" rather than on the future; and (6) traditional male/female gender role expectations.

Our immediate concern is whether this list represents stereotypes or valid, scientific generalizations. We can first point out that the list was created with good intentions by social scientists, two of whom are Latino. The features are not negative portrayals, and the authors are careful to use an academic style of writing that keeps the descriptions away from terms that might easily be considered stereotypical or even offensive. So are they stereotypes or generalizations? If you are having a difficult time deciding, then we might need to reconsider whether we can ever trust someone's else's generalizations, regardless of the intent of the authors.

But let us consider the list further: Does it do any work in helping us know more about Latinos? First, we must realize that saying anything about cultural dispositions depends entirely on a comparison with another culture. Because no "standard" culture exists, cultural description is always in relation to one or more other cultures. In this example, Latino culture is being compared with middle-class, European American culture. In fact, the authors barely mention this relation, assuming (rightly) that most readers of their article would be white, European Americans. The fact that this comparison is implicit should cause us to recognize once again the dominance of European American culture on our social institutions.

Further, it seems odd that we would agree to oppose the reification of culture at the beginning of this chapter and then move quickly to descriptions that seem static and immutable, even if they appear accurate. If such generalizations encourage us to "essentialize" the complexity, nuance, and transitory nature of culture, then we have one more reason to reconsider the value of such generalizations.

But if we can push further on these generalizations, I would like to explore one item on this list, namely the purported value that Latinos place on loyalty to and value of one's nuclear and extended family. I have my own personal history of this cultural feature: growing up bicultural has given me the advantage of seeing two sides of a cultural coin, and I can point to many differences between the ways my parents decided to manage our family life. Going to visit family on my father's side was obligatory; on my mother's it was optional. My own experiences notwithstanding, the story I would like to tell comes from a Houston, Texas, magnet high school in which I worked.

The school was located in the largely Latino east side of the city, and many of the magnet school's participants were Mexican American students; most were also girls. With the help of the school counselor, I learned that many of the female students had been offered lucrative scholarships to private universities both within and outside the state—and that few of the students accepted those scholarships. Why? Because their parents were unwilling to allow them to move away from home to attend school. I regret to say that in the minds of some of the teachers at the school, these parents were viewed as not "valuing" their child's education. I also regret to say that some developed a stereotype suggesting that Latino parents do not value education, which they seemed to apply uncritically. But this stereotype is patently false and even the generalization is not true. For these families, if young people could earn a bachelor's degree and still live at home, then that was preferable. By discouraging their children from attending exclusive universities far from home, the parents were not undervaluing education; they were simply placing great value on keeping the family intact. I want to make it clear that the families were not opposed to higher education. On the contrary, these were parents who had sacrificed greatly to make sure that their children had achieved the highest levels in secondary school. The value they placed on their children's education was beyond question, and each of their children had responded by earning several advanced placement credits and GPAs at or near 4.0. And all the students' parents encouraged them to continue their schooling at local universities. Still, it was perplexing to many of the nonimmigrant teachers at the high school who viewed the local universities as much less prestigious than those where the students had been offered scholarships. For the parents' part, university prestige played little or no part in their decision. Within these families, if you can earn a bachelor's degree and still live at home, then that is what you should do.

This example shows quite clearly how a simple generalization does not help us in understanding a complex social phenomenon. It might demonstrate that Latino families do value family relationships, but it does not suggest that such relationships are more important than education, which is how some of the teachers saw it. Like all generalizations, it fails in helping us to see culture as a process. Time and advanced education on the part of Latino parents changed their views on where to send their children for a university education. In my own extended family, my older cousins had to stay at home for college, but the younger cousins were encouraged to go away to the best school possible. As I grew to know the parents at the school better, and we developed a sense of trust, I was able to share with them the active and protective role many universities play in the safety and personal development of young people, and I believe that as a result of my interest in their children, they were more likely to agree to a residential college experience for their children. Another consistent observation is that when Latino parents gain more education themselves, they are more likely to value the enhanced educational experience a prestigious college may offer. Both examples suggest the ever-changing nature of culture and serve to limit further the value of generalizations.

Teachers are no different from anyone else in that we try to create easy categories and generalizations when the world around us is in fact a confusing, noisy place. But when we try to shortcut our way to cultural understanding through stereotypes or even employ "scientifically" derived generalizations, we miss both the complexity of our ELLs' culture and the chance to grow as cultural beings ourselves while creating a truly enriching educative experience.

CAN A SECOND CULTURE BE "LEARNED"?

We all learned a "first" culture, and learning a second takes essentially the same form, except that as adults we become burdened by our existing beliefs and practices. Because we are already versed in one culture, learning the second often places us in situations that make us feel helpless, embarrassed, or both. For example, growing up in the contemporary United States, we learned that bathing and applying deodorant daily is a routine cultural practice, although our first experience in learning it may have been

Schools have a culture all their own—one that tends to obscure the cultures students bring with them.

an embarrassing moment in middle school as teasing classmates whispered "stinky." Learning a second culture holds the same potential for unease and even shame. Cultural practices cannot be learned from a list (hence, the limits of the list of Latino cultural values I shared earlier), but truly learning the culture of our ELL students takes effort and a willingness to lay bare our ignorance.

Because schools have a culture all their own—one that tends to obscure the cultures students bring with them—acquiring culture often means spending time with students, their families, or others outside the school setting. I would like us to consider for a moment my point about school culture because, in my view, schools should promote specific values, which may or may not mesh with student culture. For instance, equity between genders is a good example of a principle that schools should consider a deeply held tradition and value, even if the culture of the students does not value gender equity in the home. Let me be clear: I am not saying that teachers should create a schooling experience that runs counter to student culture. In fact, too many schools and school systems are actually invested in obliterating students' home culture in a way that allows the dominant culture to continue to hold power. By devaluing bilingualism, certain forms of learning strategies, even some cultures' religious institutions, school systems perniciously marginalize immigrant students. In such schools, we cannot even argue the educational machinery is trying to assimilate students, urging them to lose their home culture affiliations and adopt the values of the educators who work in them. In these instances, the curriculum and instruction are designed to force immigrant students out. Like all ELD teachers, I am well aware of how the educational enterprise can be fashioned into a tool of humiliation and oppression, but my goal in this book is to describe how a teacher, perhaps working against the heaviest gears in an otherwise vicious system, can still make a difference. I might be naïve in this view, but my optimism shields my darkest doubts.

Cross-Reference For the variety of ways educators can make a difference inside and beyond the classroom, see Book 6.

The school culture at its apotheosis relies on equity, critical reasoning, and a respect for knowledge of all kinds, but even in such a school, teachers and other educators cannot disregard what students know before they cross the threshold of the school. On the contrary, teachers must understand student culture so that they can thoughtfully transition students, especially immigrant ELLs, into school culture while respecting their home culture. The only reliable way to truly understand culture is to take oneself out of the school. Visiting families' homes, as a way of acquiring culture outside the school, is a valuable idea that has been promoted by many educators. I, too, believe this approach has merit, but I have never felt comfortable inviting myself into someone's home, regardless of my position. A better strategy, to my mind, is to develop conversations with students that invite them to share their lives outside of school. As such conversations develop, teachers who show a genuine interest in students' lives may ask to attend events in the students' lives. I never once invited myself to a student's home, but after attending baseball games, church confirmations, quinciñeras, Tet celebrations, and other social events, I was invited to students' homes for birthday parties and other celebrations. And when I did visit their homes, I did so because I was genuinely invited. Furthermore, I did not consider such visits a chance to "learn" student culture; I wanted to be a part of the event. Whatever culture I acquired was secondary to a genuine desire to be among a growing circle of friends.

Teachers must understand student culture so that they can thoughtfully transition students.

I conducted a study a few years ago in which I asked six expert cooperating teachers, four of whom were Mexican American, about what their student teachers seemed to find difficult in learning to teach in their largely Mexican American classrooms (Téllez 2008). The most important idea they mentioned was the challenge in understanding the cultural viewpoints of parents and the community (i.e., culture). They sometimes misread the students, thinking that because most of them lived in poverty, they needed more love. The veteran teachers pointed out that in most cases, the children were loved plenty; yes, they needed a teacher who cared about them, but more than this they needed a teacher who had high expectations for their academic growth. One of the teachers described the process of cultural learning this way:

> The best student teachers that I have seen have become bicultural, multicultural. Not only do they learn the language, they learn about the traditions. And, you know, it's not something you are doing because you want children to learn, it is something you do because you want to. (Téllez 2008, 53)

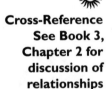

Cross-Reference See Book 3, Chapter 2 for discussion of relationships and learning theory.

To take on the learning of culture, the commitment cannot come from a professional desire; it must be personal. Not all of us are willing or able to take the time and face the potentially embarrassing task of learning a second culture, and I do not believe that we can force teachers, ELD or otherwise, to do so. It is a moral decision, and it cannot be taken lightly.

A Story of Cultural Sharing

For my part, I learned early in my career, mostly by accident, that cultural understanding was a personal challenge done out of personal desire. As I acquired Vietnamese language and culture to what I might call the "beginning intermediate" level, I came to the nascent understanding that culture was at the heart of all teaching, but not necessarily in the common and routine ways we think about it.

At the beginning of my teaching career, I had several Vietnamese students in my classes, most of whom were ELLs. As I came to know the families of my students, I began to notice that I held a fascination with, first, the language, and soon after, the culture. I also became close friends with a Vietnamese community college student,

Van, who lived in my neighborhood. This is my story of learning a new culture. I hope that it will illustrate my journey and perhaps inspire you to embark on your own.

Learning a new culture nearly always begins with a friendship, and my example is no different. Van and I first met in the alley behind my house, where my dilapidated garage served as a poor man's weight room. As a teacher, I could not justify the expense of a gym membership, so I found a used weight set, bought a boom box, and decided it was time to get in shape. After several brief "hellos," Van and I struck up a conversation, and it became clear to me that he wanted to start weightlifting. (Van later told me that he believed bigger muscles would land him a girlfriend.) I soon learned that Van had been born in Vietnam and moved to the United States when he was five, learned English in an elementary school in Santa Ana, California, and still lived with his parents. I told him that I would call whenever I had the time to work out. We soon had a regular routine, and after a month or so, we had become friends.

I admit that weightlifting might seem a stereotypical "guy" thing to do, but in retrospect it was a perfect way to get to know Van and his culture, although acquiring culture was not necessarily my intent at the beginning. First, lifting weights requires a spotter, someone who guides the weight back to the stand, especially in the common exercise known as the bench press. Trading the role of spotter and lifter develops a sound camaraderie: the lifter giving it all, and the spotter encouraging a strong effort. Second, and most important, rests in between sets of lifting offer time to talk. These talks tend to be small, nothing of great importance, but they offer more opportunities for lifters to share experiences. I suppose that other sports and activities are capable of producing such camaraderie, but weightlifting—not in a crowded gym—was key for my cultural learning.

Van and I lifted together for about a year before he moved, but through our conversations, Vietnamese culture became less of a mystery to me. In particular I learned a great deal about Vietnamese courtship rituals, past and present, or what Van called "impressing the ladies," which was why he wanted to lift weights in the first place. (By the way, Van did get in shape, but he did not find a girlfriend in the year we spent together, a fact that offers lessons beyond the scope of the book.) Of course, Van learned a great deal about U.S. culture as well, but my focus here is on what I learned. Because he was going to school, we talked about motivation for studying, why Vietnamese students were often considered a "model minority" in schools in spite of often living in poverty, and our own educational pursuits. I suppose what struck me most was how Van described the role the family—parents, grandparents, aunts, uncles, brothers, sisters—played in Vietnamese education. Later, after studying more about this role, I learned that vestiges of Confucian ideology in Vietnamese culture were responsible for the familial investment in education.

As we came to know each other better, we grew more comfortable about asking delicate questions. I recall I asked Van why most of the Vietnamese students in my class gave me wonderful gifts at the holiday and at the end of the year. Were they trying to bribe me for better grades, I asked? Van responded that bribing was not the goal. He said that giving the teacher a nice gift is just part of Vietnamese culture, but he had no idea how this practice began. Other questions about family relations, entertainment, and politics became routine topics of our conversations.

Parent night has not historically been a groundbreaking arena for culture-sharing. List some ways you can become involved with your students and their families to the point where you are sharing culture.

I share this story because it offers the only way, to my mind, that one can acquire culture. Cultural acquisition/learning must rely on a purpose that stands above gaining an understanding of the culture alone; some activity or endeavor must be the source of and motivation for cultural learning. For Van and me, the activity was weightlifting. In addition, the activity or shared purpose serves to create a bond that becomes a friendship. When friendship is driving cultural acquisition, we do not even notice that we are acquiring culture.

When friendship is driving cultural acquisition, we do not even notice that we are acquiring culture.

Learning About the Vietnamese Immigrant Population in the United States

Beginning with the families of the students in my class, my friendship with Van, and later my work in the Vietnamese community in Houston (where I also began to learn the language), my nascent understanding of Vietnamese culture grew into a scholarly study of Vietnam and Asia. Longing for a guidepost, I found Nathan Caplan, Marcella Choy, and John Whitmore's (1991) book on immigrant Vietnamese families, which suggests several features of Vietnamese culture that augmented my own understanding: (1) recognition and respect for ancestral lineage, (2) respect for elders, (3) the important role of education and knowledge, (4) cohesive and harmonious families, and (5) great regard for loyalty in all aspects of life. Again, it is important to regard these generalizations as a simplistic tool of very limited value. Indeed, I was careful not to apply them wholesale to any individual, especially to Van, for whom they rarely applied. What they did most for me was to provide a contrast to my own Mexican American/European American background. And as with any set of generalizations, I set out to find the nuances of culture that could never be contained in a list.

Taken as a whole, this list suggests that Vietnamese life is imbued with Confucian teachings and values, so the first two features are not surprising. Formally known in Asian culture as *filial piety* (i.e., worship of one's family and ancestors), the relationship between parents and children is viewed as fundamental, even metaphorical, to all life. This relationship goes well beyond the Western values that parents should love their children and that children should respect and obey their parents. The duties of children include providing their parents with physical and emotional well-being, especially in old age, but the commitment is far greater. Children have a duty to fulfill their parents' aspirations, especially in marriage and career, and do everything within their power to bring parents honor and public recognition, especially by means of academic success.

So ingrained in Vietnamese life is the concept of honor for the family that the proverb "At death a fox leaves behind its fur, humans their reputation" is commonly recited. When Vietnamese children are successful, honor comes not only to their parents but also to an entire pantheon of relatives, living and dead. In a fascinating study by My Hang Thi Nguyen (2002), a former student of mine, even Vietnamese parents who had lived in the United States for decades helped their children understand and abide by the Confucian ideals of education and knowledge.

The Vietnamese value of education and knowledge comes largely from two sources. First, the Confucian view of respect for scholars and teachers pervades Vietnamese culture. In China, from Confucius's time onward, the only way to earn a high public office was to demonstrate

Think for a moment: What are the cultural values that your parents might have passed on to you, and to what extent are they "American," or whatever country(ies) your ancestors emigrated from? How have these values affected your educational goals and ideals?

superb knowledge, and that meant scoring well on an examination of language, literature, and mathematics. (Contrast such a system with the common way to power in most Western civilizations, in which familial lineage such as royalty or, more recently, the popular vote determines government posts.) Given the importance of knowledge in Vietnamese culture, it is no surprise that teachers are very well respected. In fact, another common Vietnamese proverb maintains that "to cross a river, you must build a bridge; to have your child educated, you must love and respect the teacher."

The second source of respect for learning among Vietnamese Americans is the Buddhist influence on the society at large. While more ancient than Confucian ideology, Buddhism promotes knowledge, in one of its various forms, as a path to Enlightenment. Learning is, therefore, sacred.

As I continued to work with Vietnamese fifth- and sixth-grade students as a teacher and researcher, I quickly forgot the generalizations I had read from a book and the culture of students grew clearer to me in all its complex and wonderful ways. Specifically, I learned that providing motivation for learning was typically not necessary. I also learned that commonly held associations for doing well in school made some students uncomfortable, such as the tired "more schooling will get you more money" homily. For many Vietnamese students, this rationale cheapened the purpose of school and learning. In addition, I discovered that asking students what they wanted to be when they grew up made little sense. In some cases, the question alone caused students to be uneasy. The decision was not theirs. With this new understanding in place, I altered my classroom practices with a simple rephrasing, "What will you be when you grow up?" Years of conversations with Vietnamese friends have helped me to understand how filial piety and profound respect for parents affect school beliefs and practices, but a complete appreciation may always elude me: I am still acquiring the culture.

This is but one example of the kind of cultural knowledge that truly influences the work of teachers. When teachers are accused of promoting a "heroes and holidays" approach to culturally responsive teaching, we must respond with the ways that we alter and modify our instruction. Coming to know parents and the community takes time, but it is the only way to a genuine understanding of your ELLs.

Focus point

You may or may not choose to develop the deep cultural understanding required to act on your cultural knowledge in the classroom. I do not believe that such learning can or should be required of all teachers, but I truly hope that you will try. And in trying, remember that this is a lifetime process, because culture is in constant flux. You cannot learn a person's or a group's culture in a semester or a year.

The rewards of gaining true friends among the families of our ELLs cannot be measured in professional growth. We understand new cultures as a personal effort. For me, becoming a more culturally sensitive teacher was far secondary to the rewards of new friendships.

CULTURAL KNOWLEDGE AND THE CURRICULUM OF THE SACRED

I think that many educators would recommend that ELD teachers make a greater effort to connect the school curriculum to the lives of students. One of the most obvious expressions of connecting to ELL cultures is to use books, both fiction and nonfiction, that can represent the experiences and lives of students and their families. Although I agree with the idea in general, it seems to me that bringing "culturally bound" materials into the classroom cannot be successful until the teacher has engaged in the kind of cultural learning I have described. Without a deep knowledge of student culture, a teacher might misunderstand the "subtext" of such works (Téllez 2002). For instance, Carmen Lomas Garza paints images of her childhood growing up in south Texas. Her images

Curandera (Faith Healer). ©1989 Carmen Lomas Garza. Medium: Oil. Collection of The Mexican Museum, San Francisco, California. Used by permission of the artist.

and the text that often accompanies them are filled with memories of her childhood, and each is imbued with deep "insider" knowledge of Mexican life.

I would even call Lomas Garza's paintings *sacred.* In order for teachers to develop their students' understanding of these images, it seems to me that they must first know the cultural roots of Lomas Garza's work. In this example, the artist's family has invited a *Curandera* (a healer) into their home to help cure a sick child. Contemporary teachers of European American descent are unlikely to have a similar experience and might misunderstand the value of such a healer. True, they can learn about the tradition from students, but could mere description substitute for experience? Placing culturally rich materials in the hands of teachers and suggesting they use them with students whose experiences they believe provide a match might actually serve as a tool of humiliation. Imagine one of your own family's deepest religious traditions treated as if it were a simple fact by someone who knows little about you. Imagine yourself in a school somewhere far away: You are learning the language, and the teacher begins a lesson on Thanksgiving, a holiday that for you is filled with sacred family rituals. The teacher is describing the obvious facts about Thanksgiving (e.g., families gather to eat turkey and celebrate the Pilgrims' arrival in America) that are a part of your own family's ritual, but the teacher fails to mention the crucial importance of gathering up the extended family for the celebration or about how people fly all over the country at great expense to see one another. In other words, the teacher's explanation does not capture the sacred part of the holiday. Recognizing this shortcoming in the lesson, you try to explain it, but it is very difficult because you are learning the language.

Teachers who wish to use deeply held cultural traditions must never allow their lessons to undervalue the sacred. With this caveat I return to my earlier suggestion—that teachers learn the culture of students in the rich and highly human manner I have described before they can engage students with rich cultural materials. There are no shortcuts for this process.

CONCLUSION

Constantly changing and altering as a consequence of new ideas and new people, the culture of our students cannot be understood as an object or a learning problem. Gaining cultural knowledge might serve teachers of ELLs in a few instances, but how could we possibly learn all the cultures of all the students in our classes? If a teacher has six or seven different cultural groups in a class, and if these cultural groups shift somewhat each year, it would be almost impossible to engage in the kind of cultural immersion I have promoted. This is when generalizations may be useful, with the warning not to overuse or directly and uncritically apply them to specific children or their families.

Our immigrant ELLs deserve to have school knowledge connect in some ways to their home knowledge, but the only way to do this is for the teacher to acquire knowledge of the students' lives outside of school. Cultural acquisition takes time, but the rewards are great.

DISCUSSION QUESTIONS

1. A new teacher at your school asks about the population of Vietnamese immigrants who live in the area. Her expectation is that they will generally be quiet and respectful in class, and that they will excel in mathematics. She asks for your opinion. What will you say?

2. Think about the demographics of the students at your school now. Based on the trends revealed through statistical data in this chapter, how do you expect these demographics to change in the next ten years? How are you preparing for that change?

3. Considering your major in college, what are some ways to be culturally responsive to students of various cultures in your classroom in that content area? For example, how could you, as a biology teacher, include curricular materials that validate the culture of Mexican-descent students?

4. With a colleague, make a list of implications for your teaching practice, both in and out of the classroom, that are supported by the cultural portraits and profiles depicted in this chapter.

FURTHER READING

Cho, Yung-Ho and Jeong-Koo Yoon. 2001. "The Origin and Function of Dynamic Collectivism: An Analysis of Korean Corporate Culture." *Asia Pacific Business Review* 7, no. 4 :70–88.
  The authors describe Korean cultural values and show that Korean culture varies from other Asian cultures.
Garza, Carmen Lomas. 2005. *Family Pictures*. San Francisco: Children's Book Press.

This picture book is absolutely worth owning. Lomas Garza beautifully illustrates the life of her south Texas upbringing. She describes each painting in her own words, in both Spanish and English.

Pullum, G. K. 1991. *The Great Eskimo Vocabulary Hoax and Other Irreverent Essays on the Study of Language.* Chicago: University of Chicago Press.

This is a terrific book by my UC–Santa Cruz colleague. Highly readable, it presents a wealth of complicated linguistic theory using routine language and clever metaphors.

- The Origins of Language

- The Chomsky Challenge

- Acquisition vs. Learning

- Building the Linguistic "Placeholder"

- Meaning Is Fundamental

- Limits to Vocabulary Instruction

CHAPTER THREE

LANGUAGE ACQUISITION OR LEARNING?

N O BOOK THAT ADDRESSES the teaching of English as a new language can avoid a discussion of language: what it is, where it came from, how it is acquired, and how these foundational concerns have influenced the teaching of languages.

The discussion about language acquisition and language teaching that follows is a highly personalized account of the topic. ELD teachers who reflect on the origins and acquisition of language will be more effective language teachers. No book could possibly address all there is to know about language acquisition, so I will not bother to try. Rather, I will admit that the text follows the development of my own understanding and idiosyncratic ways of making sense of language. I am entirely convinced that ELD teachers who reflect on the origins and acquisition of language will be more effective language teachers. You must consider deeply how language seems to just "happen" for children, and the implications for teaching English as a new language. As you read this

ELD teachers who reflect on the origins and acquisition of language will be more effective language teachers.

chapter, bear in mind your own understanding of language. Is language a tool for communication only? What does language do to our consciousness? How do you, as a teacher, use language?

The first question that comes to my mind regarding language is, How did our species acquire the capacity to connect real objects to arbitrary sounds? The sound of the word *tree* has no relation to the object it represents, and yet we seem almost magically capable of creating such links between objects and ideas and random symbols and sounds. The second question is, How did our species learn to string these symbols together to make meaning? After all, we do not speak in isolated words; we speak in sentences. Moreover, we are capable of generating, even at a very young age, sentences that are completely new: they have never before been spoken. Finally, we seem to be the only species on the planet with such immense language capabilities.

As we begin to talk about language, we face a primary problem. How can we talk about language when we are already using it? As many philosophers have pointed out, how do we use the tool to understand the tool? A hammer will not be very helpful in building another hammer. Nevertheless, using language to understand language is all we have, especially in the somewhat constrained medium of a book.

I would like to consider first the origins of human language, or how our species acquired language, then move on to the dominant theory of how infants and children acquire language, and finally pull these ideas together and consider some specific strategies for teaching a second language in the classroom.

THE ORIGINS OF LANGUAGE

If we could time-travel back to central Africa about 80,000 years ago, we might be able to learn how our ancestors used a form of language that would one day become the symbol system we recognize today. If we could see how language had developed in our species, we might be able to answer thousands of questions about the role language has played in the development of thought in our species, although I suspect that we would leave with just as many new questions as answers. As it stands now, we have no record of language development. Whatever words and gestures our ancestors used are lost forever. Of course, we have samples of early writing, suggesting that the first orthographic symbol system began in China around 6,000 years ago, but certainly people were using a form of language for tens of thousands of years before the advent of writing. We have evidence of artistic forms dating back 70,000 years, which might be considered an early form of symbolic communication, but direct evidence of early spoken language cannot be discerned from the fossil record. Before orthography, or organized writing systems, we have human records of picture-symbols. (Pictographs are ancient symbols and images *painted* on the rocks; petroglyphs are ancient symbols and images scratched or *incised* into the rock surface.)

What follows is my guess about what we might have found those tens of thousands of years ago, when all *Homo sapiens* lived on the African continent (the mass migration to Asia and Europe had probably not yet begun). These early humans would be living in small tribal bands and on the verge of a flowering of technology and culture, made possible largely by the development of language.

More Important Than When: Why Did Early Humans Start Speaking?

The most fundamental question that comes to my mind is, *Which came first: language or the capacity for language? That is, did our brains develop in a way that allowed for symbolic representation, or did initial use of symbolic systems push our capacity for more language? Furthermore, how did they influence each other? If we could answer this*

Focus point

fundamental question, we would be able to describe much more comprehensively the role that language plays in our modern thinking. Knowing how language and thought developed in our species would give us an opportunity to step outside our "language-filled" minds and see how our capacity for symbolic thinking might exist independently of language.

A popular, but likely incorrect, view of the origins of language suggests that humans began using grunts and other crude vocalizations to represent objects in the environment, and then "grunted" in different ways until everybody recognized the relationship between the sound of, for example, *tree* and the object. We are easily convinced that language may have begun with vocalizations because modern humans are so dependent on speech; we cannot imagine language without it. But speech is only one symbol system that our ancestors likely employed. In fact, infants use symbolic systems based on pointing, gesturing, and even full body motions, indicating that perhaps our ancestors began to communicate using similar nonspeech symbolic systems. The development of speech was very important, however, because now we could communicate across distances ("Hey, the bison is coming your way!") and work with our hands while communicating, thus offering dramatically new communicative spaces for creating and maintaining social bonds.

Speech as a symbol system likely developed *as a consequence* of our early ability to represent objects, events, and processes using complicated gestures. The capacity to gesture (e.g., point) allowed us to get by without thousands of specific terms for objects in the environment; in other words, our language development grew as a function of thinking about how to create meaning rather than simply making sounds.

Because gestures are a perfectly appropriate way for language learners to convey meaning, especially in the beginning stages, I developed an engaging way for stu-

Think for a moment: How could you employ a teaching strategy such as this in your content area and with your students? How do you think they would react?

dents to indicate their opinion of my ideas by gesturing with their hands. Students learned that making a circular motion with their index finger next to their head meant "Mr. Téllez, your idea is crazy."

Pointing at their own head and then pointing to me meant they agreed. Putting their open hand on their forehead and shaking their head slowly meant they were exasperated with me. What began as simple gestures often grew into complex meaning-making symbol systems. Students combined gestures into complicated messages such as "I like your idea, but it is crazy." As students gained more English proficiency, I was able to use sentences to help them express their sentiment, which later served to develop their own language capacities. Gesturing is not the goal of the language teacher, but using this key communication strategy builds on the origins of language, a developmentally sensitive way to encourage meaning making. In addition, recent research studies have shown the positive relationship between gesturing and language development (McCafferty 2002).

ELD teachers must give thought to the development of language, not only as it flowers in speech but as a wider system for making meaning. Gestures draw upon our "natural" inclinations for communicating, and I have suggested that such systems are related to the development of language in humans. However, a discussion of the development of language in our species must be considered alongside one that explains how each of us, as individuals, learns language. But is *learn* even the correct term? Because we all learn our first language with such apparent ease, we must distinguish between the terms *acquire* and *learn*, and for this discussion we need the work of Noam Chomsky, who completely reshaped the way we think about the development of language.

THE CHOMSKY CHALLENGE

Noam Chomsky is likely the most widely known living social science researcher in the world. His theory of language not only altered linguistics but also has been applied in disciplines as diverse as anthropology and computer science. His political views, in which he is highly critical of the U.S. military-industrial complex, have only added to his popularity. In a recent book, Christine Kenneally (2007) suggested that "Chomsky has served as a geographic constant in the minds of generations of scientists and linguists since the early 1960s. It was as if, on the publication of his first book, he thumped down a flag and said, 'This is the North Pole,' and the rest of the scientific world mapped itself accordingly" (24–25).

Chomsky is most often credited with overturning the behaviorist paradigm in social science research when he reviewed B. F. Skinner's book *Verbal Behavior* (Chomsky 1959). In his review, Chomsky argued that language could not possibly be "learned" through operant conditioning, even via the complex role of stimuli, rewards, and patterns Skinner promoted. Language, he maintained, is largely a product of biological development, more akin to digestion than to the human activities we normally believe require learning (e.g., frying an egg, solving the quadratic formula, telling the truth). No one needs to teach an infant to digest her milk; she is already equipped with the organs needed to turn it into energy. As we grow, our digestive system changes as we take in solid foods and acquire our own individual tastes, but no one needs to learn to digest new foods. We may learn that some foods are healthier than others and eat more of those, but we do not have to learn how to digest them.

Thus, for Chomsky, language is not learned, it is *acquired*, as a natural product of biological development. In

> Think for a moment: If humans are hard-wired to acquire language from birth, what could account for the wide range of linguistic capacities sometimes seen in five-year-olds? If language is a natural part of biological development, what role does the environment play in manifold individual differences?

fact, it is impossible to stop language from happening: our brains are "hard-wired" for language. In this way, Chomsky's theory is closely connected to Piaget's more general theory of cognitive development; that is, both place great emphasis on biological development as a key feature of intellectual and linguistic growth. The environment clearly plays a role, but cognitive growth, like physical growth, is determined largely by our genetic programming.

The "Magic" of Human Languages: The Case of Word Order

Another of Chomsky's claims was that the world's languages were far more similar than we thought. He suggested that the variations in human languages, while vast at first glance, all have certain principles and general features. For instance, Chomsky and the growing number of linguists working on these questions pointed out that each human language has a specific syntax (i.e., word order within a sentence). Some languages, such as English, place the subject (S) first, the verb (V) second, and the object (O) third, resulting in the syntax pattern SVO. The syntax of the Korean language is SOV; Welsh, a language spoken in the western British Isles, is VSO. These differences do not threaten the theory because although the word order is different, they all *have* a specific syntax. Word order is the principle, not the specific order. In other words, all human languages have a specific syntax, and any child, anywhere, will acquire the syntax of whatever language is spoken around him.

Make a list of things you believe all human languages have in common. For example, all languages have sentences. What else?

A language's syntax is a guide for constructing sentences rather than a strict rule. Poets, for instance, invert the routine SVO syntax in English in order to present a thought in a unique way; Shakespeare's Macbeth utters, "So fair and foul a day I have not seen." More recently, when George Lucas created the Jedi Master Yoda for his Star Wars movies, he gave him an OSV syntax (e.g., "Always in motion the future is" or "Reckless he is"). Although average English-speaking moviegoers might not be able to name this pattern, they do recognize his speech as odd but understandable. Several websites can "translate" normal SVO English to OSV "Yoda speak." For fun, try http://www.yodaspeak.co.uk/.

Chomsky's use of the term *principle* can be roughly construed as a rule, such as whether your language uses SVO, VSO, or some other combination. The point Chomsky might want teachers to remember is that no child needed to be taught the syntax of her native language. Indeed, the vast majority of all the speakers in the world have no idea that their native language even has a syntactic pattern, just as they are unaware of how their food is digested. I would suspect this to be true even if they speak more than one language, especially if they had learned additional languages outside of a formal setting.

Do you speak or know languages other than English? What is the syntactic structure of each of those languages? If you know a computer programming language, consider its syntax.

ACQUISITION VS. LEARNING

Chomsky and his colleagues have had little to say about second-language acquisition (or is it now learning?). Can we "acquire" an L2 with the same apparent ease of our L1? Anyone who has tried to learn or teach a second language knows this is not usually the case. But Chomsky's vast influence soon found its way into L2 theory and teaching. Many L2 researchers and writers have maintained that L2 can be acquired through "natural" means, just as we acquire our first language; the most influential of these is Stephen Krashen.

Krashen's influence on L2 teaching worldwide has been great. Through his overarching theory of L2 instruction, known as the Monitor Model, Krashen (1989) essentially took the foundations of Chomsky's theory and applied it to L2 teaching. In fact, the first component of his theory explores the acquisition/learning distinction, in which he suggests that L2 is not learned but acquired. I am inclined to agree, but I tend to think that when we *teach* L2 in schools, then it makes sense to use the term L2 *learning*, and this will be our term from now on.

Another of Krashen's arguments suggests that *comprehensible input* is all that is required for L2 learning. If students can understand what is being said, they will learn the language. In fact, from Krashen's point of view, making the language, or input, comprehensible is really all that L2 teachers must do. Just as we learned our first language with input alone, so it goes with additional languages.

A further point made by both Chomsky and Krashen is the role of language output in first- and second-language development. The general argument is that the

---

Think for a moment: What is the difference between *acquiring* knowledge, especially of languages, and *learning* knowledge? Educationally speaking, when might this distinction be important?

use of language in the early stages of language development (both L1 and L2) requires input alone; that is, speaking or producing language is vastly secondary to input, at least in the beginning stages of language learning. The practical consequence for ELD teachers is that requiring ELLs to produce language—"Tell me. What's the name of this? [teacher points to an object]"—especially before they are ready, is unnecessary for language development. Such a view has vast implications for language teaching. Teachers must resist their natural inclination to find evidence of learning, and schools and the larger society must reconsider the modern desire to assess everything that is taught.

With evidence that exposure to a language is all that is needed to learn it and that the development of language in our species began with gestures as a communicating process rather than vocalizations indicating specific "words," we are prepared to consider some practical advice for ELD teachers.

One time-honored way to think about human language is to compare it to the ways that animals communicate. ELD teachers can create interesting instructional materials that help ELLs learn about animal communication. Studying animal communication also forces us to think about communication broadly, a task of particular value for ELLs. Questions such as "Does your dog understand what you say?" almost always begin a lively conversation. I have found the study of two animals—Clever Hans, a horse whose owner claimed he could do math, and Washoe, a chimpanzee who was the subject of the longest-running experiment to teach a primate a human language—serves to raise important questions about our human ability to see patterns in the environment as well as ethical questions about how we treat animals, and whether or not they can use language.

BUILDING THE LINGUISTIC "PLACEHOLDER"

If our ancestors acquired language not by first connecting individual sounds to objects but rather by communicating meaningful actions with gestures and other ways of making meaning, and if we can agree with the research showing that L1 acquisition begins not by naming things using speech, but by recognizing the events and actions in the world and gesturing (e.g., pointing) to communicate meaning, then we can draw some conclusions about how L2 teaching might benefit from a similar understanding. ELD teachers must help ELLs understand the lesson's content *before* trying to attach language to it.

The most important implication of this view is that we must have something to talk about before we can learn language. Language is acquired not by learning arbitrary terms representing objects but by growth in our cognitive capacity *for* language and the desire to understand. ELD teachers must therefore help ELLs to understand the lesson's content *before* trying to attach language to it. If we believe that the cognitive machinery had to be in place before language could be attached to the experiences of our ancestors, then it makes sense to begin with conceptual foundations of the content of what we are trying to teach, and then to add language. Such a plan often runs counter to many of our instructional instincts, which often turn toward a list of vocabulary words to be learned before actual instruction takes place.

For many ELD teachers, this is a difficult move. How can we teach language without the initial use of language? If language is our goal, how can it make any sense to begin with language-free learning? This is a fair question, but we can return to the argument about cognitive growth preceding language. If ELD teachers need to create a linguistic placeholder or "bin" for language, then using language-free materials as curriculum seems perfectly reasonable.

ELD teachers must help ELLs understand the lesson's content *before* trying to attach language to it.

Books Without Words and Teaching
Language Without Language

As I began my own ELD teaching with this view (although it was not nearly as developed as I have described here), I scoured the curricular materials in my school and district warehouses for materials that could teach without the use of language, and my first discovery was wordless picture books. Picture books are, of course, very common in the world of children's literature, and classics such as *The Snowy Day* by Jack Ezra Keats, *The Little House* by Virginia Lee Burton, or *Where the Wild Things Are* by Maurice Sendak are common when introducing young children to the purpose and value of books. These books certainly have a place in the instruction of beginning readers, for both native English speakers and ELLs alike, but the books I have in mind are less well known. They tell a compelling story without the use of any words.

One of the wordless picture book authors I find very useful is David Weisner, whose *Sector 7* provides a wonderful example of a rich and meaningful story told without any language. The story begins with a boy who befriends a cloud and then is taken to a kind of cloud factory. He helps the clouds learn to make new shapes, to the chagrin of the adults. As the young clouds experiment, they turn into the shapes of aquarium fish and ocean creatures.

The book's illustrations are superb, and the story can be read on several levels, from a simple tale of a boy who makes friends with a cloud to questions about the relationship between independence and happiness (does freedom always engender joy?). After students have "read" the book, they are free to use the language they already own to describe what happened, in writing or orally. If students need to know a word, it will come from their own desire to communicate; furthermore, the book has created a linguistic bin, a thought that precedes

Think for a moment: Probably most textbooks include bold words that can be found in a glossary at the back of the book. How can you, as an ELD instructor, approach language learning without the front-loaded emphasis on vocabulary lists, in spite of the common format found in school books?

the language needed to describe it. Word/sentence boxes and lists, completed by the teacher prior to reading the book (but not shared until the students need them), now map to existing thoughts.

Again, in this way, we create a "bin" for the new sentences as well as reasons to use them.

As I grew more convinced that creating a cognitive frame onto which language could be mapped was necessary for effective ELD, I became more convinced of the role of language-free materials for creating language learning opportunities—and I began to find additional wordless picture books. It then struck me that silent movies could serve the same purpose and possibly provide even greater context and more complex cognitive understandings. Silent movies also might be suitable for older ELLs, even adults.

Fortunately, in the history of movies we find that video technology advanced more quickly than its audio counterpart, and thus find a treasure of silent movies that deal with a wide range of humorous and complex topics. Many silent films have been restored and are available for purchase or rental from large movie distributors such as Netflix.

Although silent movies sometimes have text inserted in the footage, they largely had to rely on the camera to move the plot forward. In the best examples of silent movies, close-up shots of an actor's face reveal emotions that many modern-day movies cannot achieve with hours upon hours of dialogue. Furthermore, the topics of the films often appealed to working-class moviegoers,

Perhaps your students could make their own silent movie and later add description. They can build on the long history of the mime artist or mummer.

many of whom were immigrants in 1900–1925. There is no better example of a movie that appeals to this population than Charlie Chaplin's classic film *The Immigrant* (1917). It is also the silent film I have found most successful as an ELD teacher, especially with adult and secondary school ELLs.

The other extraordinary advantage of using wordless or speechless books or video is that they make the instructional materials equally accessible to all students, regardless of language level. In secondary ELD classrooms, which are notorious for including a very, very wide range of language learners, silent movies flatten the linguistic challenges because students do not need any language at all to understand the story: everyone gets it.

Using several different strategies, I have helped many ELD teachers introduce *The Immigrant* to their classrooms. The most common lesson includes a viewing of the movie, then inviting students to share their three favorite scenes, which they can draw and annotate with brief sentences in either English or their L1 (if they are a beginning ELL). Later, students write narratives about their own or their parents' immigration to the United States. I should point out for those who have not seen it that the movie is a comedy, but it is not without poignant moments, and these are often the scenes that grab the students' interest. The movie often compels students to share both heartbreaking and humorous stories about their early misunderstandings of U.S. culture, which I believe the movie conveys well.

Another reduced-language video that works well with younger ELLs is an excellent full-length movie that transforms Holling C. Holling's 1941 picture book *Pad-*

dle to the Sea into a superb narrative that can be easily understood without the voice-over narration of the book's text. A recent stop-motion production of *Peter and the Wolf* (Magnolia Pictures; available on iTunes) is also very good.

Creating meaningful language-free curriculum seems easiest when the topics are literature, as in the examples I have provided, but the widespread presence of video (thanks to simple tools for creating, editing, and transferring video) means that it is now quite easy for teachers to find or create video that aids ELLs in the learning of science and mathematics. For instance, one of my favorite science topics is seed dispersal, and one of the most visually appealing and informative videos on the topic comes from David Attenborough's *The Private Life of Plants*, which can be purchased from any number of online video sources (e.g., Amazon.com), but portions can also be viewed on YouTube, http://www.youtube.com/watch ?v=zbQ1jWl3AOM (at least at the time of the book's printing; such is the nature of YouTube and its ever-shifting content).

The *Private Life of Plants* episode on seed dispersal is absolutely brilliant. It shows seed dispersal in plants as widely varied as dandelions and *lianas*, which are giant vines found in Borneo. These videos cannot help to create in students the need to share their responses to the images they have seen. In the case of the liana, which lets go of its seed in the canopy of the forest using a gossamer-like wing, in particular, every student is encouraged to gesture its flight with accompanying language about the flight. A nice follow-up to this video is to challenge students to build paper airplanes that mimic the liana's seed (see below) and then conduct a flight test and record how far each "seed" traveled.

Language-free curriculum mimics the world of the L1 learner in which the context is typically at hand and children (at least in the best circumstances) are shown *how* to do things, not given explanations about why they should learn something. They watch and learn—mostly by listening—and later, sometimes much later, use language to describe the experience.

Teachers must consider that the advantage of such materials goes well beyond providing a simple context: Language-free curricula democratize the classroom by offering all students access to a wide range of complex narratives or scientific information.

MEANING IS FUNDAMENTAL

The notion of making instruction meaningful will strike many teachers as a prosaic recommendation. Of course instruction must be meaningful for our learners. If it has no meaning for them, they will not understand. Of course teachers must create meaning by connecting new information to what their students already know, whether that means making connections to yesterday's lesson or to students' deep cultural knowledge. Meaningful school knowledge is a clear enough goal, but finding its exact place is challenging. However, meaningful instruction must have its due. For the ELD teacher, the focus on meaning takes on an even more important role. In order to understand why, we can begin with an exploration of first-language acquisition.

For infants and children learning their first language, what are the important features of this input? We lack the space here for a full discussion of the features of linguistic input in L1 acquisition, but we can identify a few primary features. For instance, Michele Shady and Louann Gerken (1999) suggest that sensitive adult caregivers provide strategic *prosodic* changes, such as pausing, syllable lengthening, and pitch resetting, at the boundaries of noun and verb phrases. So in the sentence "The caterpillar ate two leaves," the careful speaker is likely to pause after "caterpillar," thus allowing the infant to notice the subject of the sentence. *Prosody* is the term to de-

Key concept
prosody

scribe those features of language that express meaning beyond the actual sentences and words used.

Though these prosodic cues are important, what is more important is that this sentence would very likely be spoken in reference to a picture book in which the caregiver would be pointing to the caterpillar while using these prosodic strategies. An even more contextual event might find the caregiver and infant in the garden, watching a caterpillar eating leaves. In this scene, the context is even more immediate.

Speech directed toward infants and young children displays special characteristics, such as heightened pitch, exaggerated intonation, and increased repetition of words and clauses, that differ from the speech adults use with one another. Such "motherese" or "infant-directed talk" is typical of fathers as well as mothers, nonparents as well as parents, and across diverse ages and socioeconomic groups. What we do not notice in any studies of "motherese" is any particular attention to the form of the language. Parents/caregivers do not seem to limit their input to any particular context, tense, or vocabulary. In fact, very early on, they seem to use stories or narratives without any regard to how difficult it might be for the child to understand. As long as they believe the story has meaning for the child, it is told.

It is this complete attention to meaning, regardless of the complications or displaced language, that seems to be the most striking feature of speech to infants or young children. Parents and other caregivers may repeat,

Think for a moment: How could you, as an ELD instructor, communicate meaning to learners who are too old to benefit from motherese? What might you need in a classroom to more effectively make meaning with students who speak another language?

rephrase, or gesture, but their focus is always on communicating *meaning*.

It is unnecessary to point out rules of language to a young child. She will learn them with ease, in spite of the fact that she has no conscious knowledge that she is using any rules at all. No caring parents—save for a few over-enthusiastic linguists!—would ever take the time to explain irregular verb tenses in English to their two-year-old, and yet every two-year-old who hears English will quickly acquire the distinction between "I am eating my lunch now" and "I already ate my lunch." This simple fact convinced Chomsky and later the linguistic research community that our capacity for language must be largely innate. But language acquisition happens as a result of a flood of (meaningful) linguistic input.

Focus point *Could part of the reason we learn a first language with such ease be that perhaps infants and young children are not focused on learning the language but rather on understanding what is being said? One way to think about this is that ELD teachers must re-create the world of the child learning a first language, with the highly complicating addition of teaching academic tasks as well as reading and writing, neither of which naturally emerges without specific instruction.* In Chapter 6, we will explore some of the psychological consequences of this arrangement, but for now we will focus only on pedagogical and linguistic concerns.

Imagine a middle-school Algebra I class, half of whom are ELLs. The teacher of such students is faced with the task of helping students to learn (1) the mathematical concepts of algebra, (2) the specific academic language associated with Algebra, and (3) enough generalized English skills to make sense of the lessons. Pedagogically, one of the most important goals in Algebra I is the mastery of simple linear equations, and there is no shortage of paper-and-pencil strategies for learning this concept. A thoughtful ELD/math teacher could use any number of them and likely be successful. However, if we push our pursuit of making meaning into a lesson on linear equations, we might imagine a teacher inviting the students to use Texas Instruments graphing calculators equipped with an inexpensive sensor that can measure water salinity. A field trip to a local estuary invites the students to take salinity readings at various points along a river right up until it empties into the ocean. Back in the classroom, the students plot their readings and create a curvilinear equation that can be used to predict the river's salinity based on distance from the ocean. Later, they can make predictions about which fish could live at various points. They might also explore how climate change would influence the wildlife in the estuary as sea levels rise. Perhaps they would share their data with local environmental groups who are working to protect the estuary.

In the previous example, meaningful instruction, or teaching with a real purpose in mind, dominates the lesson. The ELL students are not required to guess about how linear equations might be used; the deeply embedded context provides all the meaning they would need. Walking along the river, touching the water (perhaps even tasting it), recording data, and observing the wildlife make learning algebra and English a far easier task. As with a caregiver talking about a caterpillar, meaning is foremost.

The notion of packing a lesson with meaning recalls one of Krashen's principles: he claimed that L2 learning could be made subconscious if students were so completely focused on what was being said that they would forget they were learning in an unfamiliar language. Although this part of Krashen's theory has been contested and admittedly lacks an extensive research base, our example provides a plausible explanation. If ELLs are so

---

In fact, there are algebra applications practically everywhere. Can you think of some other meaningful activities for students to try, both in and out of the classroom, using math?

The brain's capacity for learning language is greatest when we are also learning content.

entirely focused on the work at hand, and they are learning volumes of content in English, it is entirely likely that their attention to the project will "bury" the fact that it is not their native language. In addition, we have some preliminary evidence that the brain's capacity for learning language is greatest when we are also learning content; that is, learning about the world. This is the hallmark of first-language acquisition, so, to my mind, it makes perfect sense that we learn a new language best when we forget we are learning it all. ELD teachers, then, should do all they can to disguise language teaching within meaningful lessons and create learning conditions in which the language of instruction is transparent. As an ELD teacher, you must devote the vast majority of your attention to meaning in your instruction. If your planning is accurate, the content level appropriate, and your students engaged, language will magically rise to the occasion.

LIMITS TO VOCABULARY INSTRUCTION

Key concept
vocabulary instruction

When confronted with ELD, most teachers, quite understandably, are drawn to strategies that help their students understand the meaning of words, what we often call **vocabulary instruction**. As my colleague Judith Scott has suggested, the term *vocabulary instruction* implies a simplistic approach to word meaning; she instead favors the term *word consciousness,* which implies myriad links among words and their meanings.

I have never been able to forget the words of Gottlob Frege, a nineteenth-century philosopher and mathematician, who said: "Never ask for the meaning of a word in isolation, but only in the context of a sentence." I have spent the better part of the past decade or so wondering what this might mean for L2 teaching.

For Frege, who I will admit never wrote anything about L2 teaching, the sentence is the unit of thought, and thus no word has meaning unless it is surrounded by a context.

Using the sentence as the essential unit of language may draw us away from the obvious challenge for ELLs: they need to know the meanings of words if they are to understand language. I wholly agree, but I have made the shift from asking ELLs "What does this word mean?" to "What does this sentence mean?" The results of this approach promote student focus on comprehending the sentence rather than simply trying to recall a definition.

I admit to having only anecdotal accounts of the success of this way of teaching, but a few research studies seem to bear out the strategy. The first evidence comes from neurobiological studies that indicate that our brain is wired for both syntax and sentence meaning. For instance, in a recent study, Mirella Dapretto and Susan Bookheimer (1999) found that highly specialized regions of the brain are associated with syntactic understanding and semantic meaning but discovered no such specific architecture for word knowledge. Our knowledge of words seems to be much less specific. This finding is not surprising: sentences, not words, do the work of communicating.

Many teachers have made extensive use of *word walls* as a tool for developing language. Though they take many forms, the general idea is that providing students with the written form of common words will develop language. I agree that word walls are an important tool for ELD classrooms, but I would also suggest that ELD teachers follow the advice of Karen Carrier and Alfred Tatum (2006) and add *sentence walls* to their rooms. They suggest using "cloze" sentences from content instruction that require a fill-in word from a word wall (e.g., "When the sun heats surface water, the water _____"). I would also suggest that teachers place useful sentences spoken or written by the students themselves on the wall. For instance, beginning language learners need chunks of language to help them negotiate the L2 world. Phrases such as "Can I play, too?" are very useful for young beginning language learners.

CONCLUSION

I have tried to draw upon a wide range of language concepts to inform a few ways we might reconsider the ways we teach L2 learners. The development of language in our species suggests that gesturing may have played an important role in later (oral) language use. The growth of speech was made possible by our capacity for using gestures (1) to represent objects not in the immediate context, and (2) to describe processes rather than just objects. Once we had developed the cognitive ability to do both, it was an easy step to use oral speech for most communication. Speech then offered a number of advantages, but speech also came as a consequence of our ability to make meaning via gestures and other communicative acts. We must keep in mind the principles of early language learning. If we did not require specific linguistic instruction in acquiring our first language, why should we need it in "learning" our second? Although we have very compelling examples of people who have learned additional languages without instruction, it is most often the case that these people have learned only the spoken form of the language and have not been asked to learn academic terms and phrases.

DISCUSSION QUESTIONS

1. In what ways is learning a second language similar to learning a first language? How are they different? What might be the implications for teachers, given these similarities and differences?

2. What are some ways to use language-free materials in various content areas? How can you employ these methods in your own classroom?

3. What are the dangers of teaching language as a list of vocabulary words? What methods might work better in your own classroom?

4. Create a list of things you believe to be true about language acquisition and language learning, and then share it with a colleague. Does she agree with you on all points? Does she have anything new to add to your list?

FURTHER READING

Gould, Stephen J. 1977. *Ontogeny and Phylogeny.* Cambridge, MA: Belknap Press.

One of the country's most famous naturalists, Gould (1941–2002) made complex evolutionary concepts easily understandable. This book is a bit more technical than his other writings, but educators will likely find it very compelling, as Gould connects ideas as varied as human evolution and the school curriculum.

Ortega, Lourdes. 2009. *Understanding Second Language Acquisition.* Oxford: Oxford University Press.

A highly readable book in the field of theoretical second-language acquisition, a genre that I find generally to be pretty boring. Ortega addresses topics such as motivation from a fresh perspective that I believe ELD teachers will find both interesting and helpful.

Searchinger, Gene. 1995. *The Human Language.* Series. Equinox Films, Inc.

Many university libraries have this three-part documentary, but it may now be out of print. It describes language and language learning in a thoughtful but light-handed way and includes interviews with many famous linguists.

- History of Bilingual Education in the United States

- Bilingual Education vs. ELD Instruction

- Modern Bilingual Education

- Measuring Language Instruction Effectiveness

- Creating a Supportive Language Environment

- The Promise of Code-Switching

- Two-Way Immersion

CHAPTER FOUR

BILINGUAL EDUCATION, ELD, AND THE DEBATE

BILINGUAL EDUCATION MAY BE the most controversial educational program in the United States. Myth and misunderstanding surround its purpose and actual practice. What many have viewed, incorrectly, as an educational program designed to teach Spanish (or another language) is in fact a strategy to help students learn to read in English more quickly. As ELD or bilingual teachers, we must face squarely the theory and research on bilingual education and decide where we fit along the continuum of views on native-language instruction. Using a student's native language clearly has a place in educating ELLs, but I think that the field has been narrow-minded in the ways that we have interpreted what bilingual education is and can achieve. The purpose of this chapter is to reappraise what we know about the effects of bilingual education. Not surprisingly, we begin with a story rooted in politics.

Sometime in 1995, Ron Unz, a wealthy businessman from northern California, took on an unusual political campaign. Using his significant financial resources and California's wide-open rules for putting propositions on the statewide ballot, Unz managed to put a pedagogical practice up for a vote, the first time ever in the nation's history.

With the passage of Proposition 227 in 1997, bilingual education—the instructional program that uses a child's native language to teach initial literacy skills and other content (and later transitioning students to an all-English curriculum)—was severely curtailed. The Unz bill went far in circumscribing the instructional programs schools could provide for their ELLs. For instance, prior to the bill's passage, a student who spoke a language other than English at home was, by default, put into a bilingual education classroom, provided the school could provide instruction in the native language of the student. Parents who did not wish to have their children in a bilingual program were required to sign a release stating that they had chosen to forego the bilingual program. After Proposition 227, schools could still offer bilingual education, but they were required to obtain special state approval. More important, the default placement for ELL students was in an ELD class, and parents who wanted their child in a bilingual program, if it was available, were required to come to the school, sign a document, and opt their child *into* bilingual education.

The upshot of the passage of Proposition 227 is that California schools or school districts wanting to discard their bilingual programs have been able to do so with ease. Schools committed to bilingual education have continued their programs in spite of additional bureaucratic mandates, but the political fallout has continued unabated (Galindo 2004). Unz successfully brought similar initiatives to other states, most notably Arizona, where restrictions on native-language instruction are even greater than those mandated in California.

I raise the issue of Proposition 227 because it underscores a tension that ELD teachers must address: Does being an ELD teacher imply that one is opposed to bilingual education? Does being an ELD teacher suggest that one does not value ELLs' native languages? The obvious and easy answer to both questions is no, but a genuinely reflective answer is much more complicated and requires us to think carefully about our position on native-language instruction.

I will quickly follow these comments by saying that I recognize that bilingual teachers are also ELD teachers. Bilingual programs should be just that: bilingual. Therefore, every bilingual teacher in the United States will include ELD instruction as part of the curriculum. I also want to point out that although this book's focus is on ELD teachers, I myself have worked in bilingual education and ELD programs and believe that bilingual education, when implemented properly, is very effective. Nevertheless, most ELD teachers are not bilingual teachers. Should we feel guilty?

Generally, I find that ELD teachers are not opposed to native-language instruction, although I know some ELD teachers who do not favor bilingual education. Such teachers feel no remorse at all: ELD works just fine, and native-language instruction is unnecessary. In my view, these teachers have not reflected on either the theory or research in language education and have not considered their position very seriously.

Consider for a moment your own linguistic capacity and that of your students. It is unlikely that you are able to speak all of the languages used by your students. Given that, have you ever felt inadequate as a teacher for not knowing those languages? Or have you felt it was a strength, compelling you to try harder to make lessons meaningful for your students, knowing that you would not be able to express your ideas in their native languages?

HISTORY OF BILINGUAL EDUCATION
IN THE UNITED STATES

What ELD teachers must realize is that the debate over the value of bilingual education has grown well beyond academic concerns, and as Proposition 227 has pointed out, the politics of bilingual education makes it a very serious issue indeed. But politics has always been a central feature of bilingual education. Early forms of bilingual education in the United States (c. 1850) were common in midwestern communities where German and English were taught side by side (Kloss 1977). The start of World War I, which saw the United States mobilized against the Central Powers of Germany and Austria, abruptly ended German-language instruction in U.S. schools.

More recently, Title VII of the 1964 Civil Rights Act outlawed discrimination by race, color, religion, sex, or national origin and further provided federal funds so that schools could address the needs of students for whom English was not their first language. Although Title VII provides resources needed for the growth of bilingual programs, it does not specify that language instruction must begin in the child's native language. In 1971 the State of Massachusetts legislated a program of bilingual education for native Spanish speakers at the urging of Spanish-speaking parents. Other states followed suit. In 1974 a group of Cantonese-speaking parents in San Francisco argued their case for native-language instruction all the way to the Supreme Court. In *Lau v. Nichols,* the parents maintained that their children, who spoke only Cantonese but who were being placed in classrooms where only English was spoken, did not understand what was being taught. The plaintiffs argued that the children's civil rights had been violated because they were denied equal access to the curriculum under Title VII, which prohibited any discrimination based on national origin, among other relevant categories (see Stewner-

Think for a moment: Are there any bilingual education programs in your local schools? What are the arguments you have heard from other teachers or in your community for or against bilingual education?

Manzanares 1988 for an overview of the legal and legislative history of bilingual education).

Lau v. Nichols rendered bilingual education the only viable option for schools that had at least twenty students who spoke a language other than English. Consequently, school districts quickly implemented bilingual programs but were immediately confronted by teacher shortages. As might be expected, bilingual programs met with great resistance in many areas where communities grew suspicious of a program that did not immediately teach students English.

As school districts struggled to implement quality bilingual education programs, and a growing number of shrill policymakers continued to criticize the *Lau* decision, the Bilingual Education Act of 1984 allowed for and, perhaps more important, funded special alternative instructional programs in which the native language need not be used, but one in which English-language instruction and special instructional services are provided to facilitate achievement of English competency. This is why schools in the United States receive about $120 per "LEP" student, as long as those students are receiving an approved program.

As the historical record illustrates, bilingual education has always been tightly coupled to the notion of students' civil rights. Those who conceive of bilingual education as a matter of social justice are common, and no writer of this persuasion is more widely read than Jim Cummins. Cummins (1986) introduced a large audience to Wallace Lambert's concept of additive and subtractive language policies. For Cummins, language education without bilingual education is subtractive, tantamount to the removal of students' native language and replacing it with the society's dominant language. More radical commentators have invoked the horrors of the past (e.g., Indian Schools in the United States) and freely used terms such as *linguistic genocide* to draw an even sharper comparison between programs that teach in the native language and others that teach only in the target language (Skutnabb-Kangas 2000). With teaching framed in such stark terms, it is no wonder that many ELD teachers approach their work with moral misgivings, worried that teaching English alone might erode their students' native languages and perhaps undervalue their culture.

For my part, I wholeheartedly support quality bilingual education, but I am also convinced that ELD instruction, when done well, is not subtractive in the way Cummins and others have argued. In explaining my position, the first task at hand is to consider the research on bilingual and ELD education. This is admittedly a troublesome and sometimes tedious topic, capable of drawing us into important but highly technical research methodologies and complicated language-testing topics. I will try to keep the focus on the larger concepts, but exploring the research is crucial to developing a critical view on the benefits of native-language instruction. As I mentioned, we must decide where to place ourselves along the continuum of support for native-language instruction and then defend that position. Consider where your own ideas lie on a continuum that supports L2 instruction that does or does not include students' native languages. To some extent, your ideas may be influenced by how many non-English languages you speak, if any. A teacher in the United States whose native language is not English surely has some strong and well-supported opinions on this topic. What is the range of positions?

BILINGUAL EDUCATION VERSUS ELD INSTRUCTION

Before we can address the question of what research can tell us about the relative merits of bilingual and ELD instruction, we need to provisionally define bilingual education and the specific programs that have emerged from the general category. For a moment, I would like to put aside the potential cultural and social advantages of knowing two or more languages, and concentrate only on the linguistic or cognitive rationale for bilingual education.

The theoretical foundation of bilingual education is based partly on an adaptation of Roger Brown's iceberg theory of linguistic knowledge (Brown 1973). This theory suggests that the vast majority of our knowledge of a language exists below the conscious level at which we actually use our language, just as the bulk of an iceberg is below the surface of the water and out of sight. Brown's theory suggests that this "deep structure" of language knowledge is quite general and not rooted in any single language.

A similar idea was proposed in the nineteenth century by the French linguist Ferdinand de Saussure, who used the term *langue* to represent one's "collective" knowledge of language. *Parole* designates individual speech acts, statements and utterances, and events of language use. Parole, therefore, refers to how we *use* language. Bilingual education theorists argue that language development *in any language* will enhance our deep knowledge of language (langue) and therefore helps one to become more competent in all linguistic tasks, whether they are in our native language or one that we are learning.

Key concept
langue

Cummins adapted the iceberg metaphor by suggesting that linguistic knowledge for two (or more) languages springs from a single "well"; that is, we do not have separate meaning systems for multiple languages. And here we find the linchpin of bilingual education.

Development in a child's native language, especially in literacy, does not detract from learning to read and write in a second language. On the contrary, the theory suggests that more development in L1 enhances competence in L2. Therefore, if we begin literacy instruction in students' native languages, the reading skills and concepts gained in the first language transfer to reading skills in the second language, although a few studies have shown that this transfer is in fact quite complicated and does not necessarily happen on its own (Hardin 2001).

MODERN BILINGUAL EDUCATION

At its core, bilingual education is designed to provide access to the school curriculum using the students' native languages almost exclusively in the early stages of schooling. As students matriculate through the bilingual education program, their use of the native language is reduced and the dominant language increases until all instruction is provided in the "majority" language. In the U.S. context, the vast majority of bilingual education programs provide native Spanish-speaking children with academic content and literacy instruction in Spanish. Each successive year in the program relies more and more on the delivery of academic content in English until around the fifth year of schooling, when students have "transitioned" into all-English instruction. *The key issue in bilingual education is the timing of the transition to instruction in L2.* Bilingual programs are therefore often referred to as early- or late-exit. **Early-exit bilingual programs** seek to transition students out of native language instruction as soon as they meet the exit criteria, sometimes as early as the first grade. **Late-exit programs** typically encourage students to receive native language instruction after they have met the exit criteria. Interestingly, school-based programs that continue to develop students' L1 after they have gained competence in L2 are very rare.

Focus point

Key concepts
early-exit
and *late-exit*
bilingual
programs

Think for a moment: Who writes and decides on exit criteria for ELLs? Is it the same criteria for native speakers of all languages? Should it be so? As an ELD teacher, what skills and qualities would you require of students if you could decide on their exit into mainstream academic instruction?

When we understand these programmatic features, Unz's success in legislating an end to opt-in bilingual education is all the more puzzling. After all, the goal of bilingual education has always been to move students into instruction in the dominant language (e.g., English). Native-language instruction was intended to serve only as a "bootstrap" for learning L2 and content.

MEASURING LANGUAGE INSTRUCTION EFFECTIVENESS

So what does the research tell us about the effects of ELD and bilingual education? Which method—ELD or bilingual education—more quickly leads to oral and literacy skills in English? This seems like a straightforward research question, but measuring the effects of bilingual education provides cases replete with evaluation challenges regarding the definition of programs, misattribution of effects, and, in the following case, disagreements about where one program starts and another begins. When the U.S. Department of Education funded the Bilingual Immersion Evaluation Project (Ramirez et al. 1991), it believed that the educational community would finally have its answer on which type of language education was best for native Spanish-speaking children. Briefly described, the Immersion Report studied three programs—structured English immersion (ELD), early-exit bilingual education, and late-exit bilingual education—an attempt to uncover which of the three was most effective in teaching English literacy. In general, the study found that

The development of language is arguably the widest goal of schooling, at least for young children.

late-exit programs were most effective. But no sooner had the report been released than a panel of experts was convened by the National Research Council to review the findings (Meyer and Fineberg 1992). The experts were charged with the task of evaluating the report's program coherency, the overall research design, and the statistical analysis. In the end, the panel suggested, among other things, that the three treatment groups were in fact versions of the same treatment and that two of the treatment groups were "indistinguishable from one another" (102). The panel concluded by arguing that no implications about the effectiveness of the language education models in the study should be drawn from the Immersion Report. The development of language is arguably the widest goal of schooling, at least for young children.

The Immersion Report example is merely one example among many evaluation reports on bilingual education, but its story is not uncommon. The marking of a program as a specific instructional "packet," as something different from what is normally carried out by a school, is very difficult, especially when we are concerned with the study of educational programs that revolve around the teaching of language. The development of language is arguably the widest goal of schooling, at least for young children, so it is not surprising when evaluators and educators find it hard to isolate program effects. Nevertheless, controlling program effects when the most important feature of program implementation—the teachers themselves—remains largely outside the program implementation design is yet another challenge faced by educational programmers. Educational evaluators must admit that even the most ill-conceived program models can succeed in the hands of expert teachers who are capable of bending programs to meet student needs. Even so, carefully designed programs can fail when teachers do not understand clearly the program purpose or are unable to carry out its design.

Think for a moment: What are the ethical considerations when trying to study various educational reforms? Would you volunteer your child to be part of the group that receives experimental instruction? Or, more important, would you want your child to be part of the control group, which might, in some cases, receive no instruction at all while others are receiving reforms believed to be helpful?

Following publication of the Immersion Report and the subsequent review by the National Research Council, the field has been overwhelmed with research, or rather mostly summaries of research, that have sought to find an answer to the relative merits of bilingual education versus ELD. These recent studies have tried to avoid the problems associated with critiques of the Immersion Report by examining only those studies with clear distinctions between the programs. Although I do not want to draw us into a review of the dozens of such studies, I would like to share the results of a recent article by Kelly Rolstad, Kate Mahoney, and Gene Glass (2005) as an authoritative answer to the question. Bear with me; we are going to be using some statistical reasoning, and the results of their research, though authoritative, are not definitive. These researchers complied the results of about thirty previous studies of bilingual and ELD programs (most assessed effects at about the third grade) and found that the "effect size" on English literacy scores of students who participated in bilingual education versus ELD was +.23. This means that the students in bilingual education outperformed those students in ELD programs on an English test. So now we have it, right? Bilingual education is more effective. Unfortunately, the picture is not so clear. If you know just a tiny bit of statistics, understanding effect size is easy. First, I can tell you that effect size can be interpreted in standard deviation units, so an effect size of +.23 means a difference of about 9 percentile points. Imagine two ELL kindergarten students who are both average and equal in every way. One starts in bilingual education, the other in an ELD program. At the end of third grade, the bilingual student's percentile score on the English literacy test stands at 59 points whereas the ELD student's score is 50 percentile points. Still no contest, right? Bilingual education is the clear winner. Sorry—again—to complicate the picture. Although the study found a difference, we cannot necessarily attribute this difference to the effects of the programs. It is not a large enough difference to be conclusive. Other factors, such as teacher quality or the availability of good curricula, which were out of the control of the researchers who conducted the original studies, could be responsible for the difference in test scores.

Even with all the caveats of this research in place, we can safely conclude that high-quality bilingual programs are as good and perhaps even a little better than ELD programs in advancing English literacy development. For those who would critique bilingual education as ineffective in promoting English, they have no defensible position.

A recent large-scale study in California attempted to uncover the effects of Proposition 227. Had the elimination of bilingual education curtailed native Spanish-speaking ELL achievement? California offered a unique opportunity to assess the effectiveness of ELD versus bilingual education because many schools sought waivers to retain bilingual education and thus offered a comparison group. Although substantial methodological challenges had to be overcome, a recent 225-page report by two independent research groups found that

> bilingual instructional approaches were not statistically different from structured English immersion [ELD] approaches in improving ELL performance. *Our overall conclusion, based on the data currently available, is that there is no clear evidence to support an argument of the superiority of one EL instructional approach over another.* (italics in original) (Parrish et al. 2006, ix)

Think for a moment: Let's say you are having a conversation in the teacher's lounge with a non-ELD teacher who is against bilingual education. What would you say in support of bilingual education? Can you use some of the research cited in this chapter to support your argument?

Although the type of program was not found to be significant, the report found that the *quality* of the program was crucial, maintaining that four features of the language teaching program produced the highest academic gains: (1) staff capacity to address EL needs; (2) schoolwide focus on English-language development and standards-based instruction; (3) shared priorities and expectations in regard to educating ELLs; and (4) systematic, ongoing assessment and data-driven decision-making.

Let's return now to our original question: based on research alone, should ELD teachers feel guilty for not using native-language instruction? It seems that bilingual programs might have a slight advantage in promoting English literacy skills and have a clear, obvious advantage when it comes to developing native-language literacy skills. Such an advantage might be reason enough for ELD teachers to be dubious of their own role in language education, but it is important to remember that most immigrant families lose some or all of their native-language by the third generation. We might also be reminded that few ELLs, other than native Spanish-speaking students, ever had the opportunity to receive native-language instruction because either their numbers were too small or the school could not find teachers who spoke their language, and yet many have been successful in school. Of course, we do not know if these students would have been more successful if they had experienced bilingual education.

Given the largely positive effects of bilingual education, how has Ron Unz been able to get voters to prohibit such programs? The answer is complicated, but it appears to be related to our "sloganeer" political culture, in which explanations about effect sizes, for instance, have no chance of informing the public debate (Téllez, Flinspach, and Waxman 2005). In the end, I suppose that we each will have our own answer, which will be based partly on the research but mostly on other factors.

CREATING A SUPPORTIVE LANGUAGE ENVIRONMENT

Even if we agree that ELD instruction is comparable to bilingual education with regard to achievement in English, I am certain that the vast majority of ELD teachers would choose to endorse their students' home languages and cultures even if they do not use students' L1 as an instructional medium.

Achieving this goal is challenging but not impossible. ELD teachers, as I have shared, should first begin the acquisition of the culture of their students. Along with gaining a deep understanding of culture, learning the language of the students' families is important. In fact, a good goal for any ELD teacher is to speak the language of the students well enough to conduct parent conferences or make a phone call with the assistance of, but not total reliance on, a translator. With some effort, this level of proficiency can be gained in a few years of dedicated study. My recommendation for this task is to find a parent or set of parents at the school who are interested in helping to tutor you in the language. Perhaps you can trade English tutoring for learning their language, or payment of $15–25 an hour is probably fair. I would recommend holding the tutoring sessions at the parents' home for convenience. This also allows you to make "home visits" with a genuine purpose in mind. Search the Web for some instructional materials that will help you and the parents. Have them teach you some sentences that relate to schooling to get you started, be patient with your tutors and yourself, and work on communicating rather than mastery. In a year or two, you'll be very surprised how much you can say.

Do not make "fluency" or expert speaking your immediate goal. I have found so many teachers whose lack of proficiency in ELL native languages holds up perfection in the L2 as their goal. I think these overly high expectations have prevented many English-speaking teachers of ELLs from using the students' native languages altogether. Using the most common example, I think that many ELD teachers believe that learning Spanish seems like an impossible task. But why is this belief widespread? These are teachers who see daily the largely positive results of their own language instruction. You will probably find that parents are very forgiving of your language development.

THE PROMISE OF CODE-SWITCHING

It is my view that *many ELD teachers may have had a debilitating experience in high school or university foreign language classes and thus consider a second language too difficult to learn.* Of course, the pursuit of academic proficiency in any second language requires extensive effort, but the use of certain words can be sprinkled within English in a process called code-switching. Code-switching can be an effective way to begin to learn a language while also creating solidarity with ELLs, thereby endorsing home language and culture while the teacher learns the language of the students (Nichols and Colón 2000). Strategic code-switching can both assist the ELD teacher in learning the language and create a cultural connection with students, provided the language "mixing" is done carefully. *Code-switching* is a linguistics term denoting the concurrent use of more than one language, or language variety, in conversation. Multilinguals, people who speak more than one language, sometimes use elements of multiple languages in conversing with each other. Thus, code-switching is the syntactically and phonologically appropriate use of more

Focus point

**Key concept
code-switching**

than one linguistic variety. Two or more speakers may practice code-switching when they are each fluent in both languages. In the 1940s and the 1950s many scholars called code-switching a substandard language usage. Since the 1980s, however, most scholars have recognized it as a normal, natural product of bilingual and multilingual language use.

Before addressing the process of classroom code-switching for teachers, I would like to explore Michael Halliday's theory of language functions, which I hope will provide a context and rationale. He suggests that language has seven functions, each with a specific task (see Table 4-1).

ELD teachers will quickly recognize the instrumental and informative functions of language. The centrality of language as a resource for the conveying of information suggests that teachers who are not highly proficient in the language of instruction should not use this function. After all, how can a teacher communicate ideas to students without a deep knowledge of that language? A teacher with limited capacity in a language may model incorrect language forms for ELLs.

Yet other language functions offer alternatives to using the native language of the students. All of us understand how children and parents rely on a nearly limitless flow of language as they negotiate their roles, test the limits of each other's power, and, most important, express love and care. The interactional function of language, which provides the social cohesion required for any community,

Table 4.1   Michael Halliday's Language Functions and Tasks

Instrumental	Language for the work of life, to satisfy needs and wants
Regulatory	Language for social control
Interactional	Language for the establishment of social relationships
Personal	Language to create a "self-text"
Imaginative	Language to express and fantasize
Heuristic	Language as a tool for learning about the world
Informative	Language for the conveyance of information

cannot be overlooked. *My proposition is that ELD teachers can learn to code-switch with their students' native languages by using terms of endearment and other interactional functional phrases that serve to validate home culture and language while not requiring advanced proficiency.* Using a Spanish dialect from Mexico and some Central American countries as an example, ELD teachers can quickly learn a few terms of endearment to get started with the language and create a supportive environment for their students. Much in the way teachers use terms such as "honey," "kiddo," or "friend" with students, they may create a stronger social relationship with their Spanish-speaking students by using terms of endearment familiar to Mexican children and youth. It is important to point out that some teachers do not use terms of endearment with their students in any language. If this is the predilection of a teacher, then using terms of endearment in the students' L1 may sound forced or uncomfortable. I know many native Spanish-speaking teachers who do not use any such terms with their Mexican American students. Therefore, I am not making the case that using terms of endearment is required by teachers to create a culturally supportive environment, but rather their use serves as just one example of the use of interactional language in students' L1.

Focus point

In Mexico, for instance, the most common term of endearment by far is *mijo* or *mija,* a contraction of *mi* ("my") and *hija/o* ("son/daughter"). Although the literal translation is son/daughter, the term is often used by adults who are not the child's parents. However, *mija/o* is probably not appropriate for older students unless the teacher knows them very well. For middle and secondary students, *compañero/a* is a useful term of endearment that translates roughly as "partner," as in partner in learning.

Many other terms, such as *amorcito* ("little love"; similar to "sweetheart"), will be commonly used by parents but perhaps not by teachers. The best way to know which terms might be best suited to a particular age and region is to listen carefully to parents and perhaps other

All teachers can develop a genuine relationship with their students while supporting their native language.

teachers. Again, however, if a teacher would not use terms of endearment with native English-speaking students, forcing terms of endearment in another language will sound strained.

As ELD teachers develop a relationship with their students, they might choose to sprinkle such terms into their interactions with students. By using the native language and dialect of ELL communities, all teachers can develop a genuine relationship with their students while supporting their native language. Teacher-educators may also find useful a dictionary of words in the Mexican American dialect of Spanish. Adolfo Ortega (1991) provides a dictionary of words of the particular dialect of Spanish associated with Mexican Americans.

In our other primary L1 example, Vietnamese, terms of endearment present a completely different picture. Vietnamese parents, relying on ancient beliefs, will sometimes use disparaging terms with their children and call them "stupid" or "ugly" so that the evil spirits will not be attracted to them. Although contemporary Vietnamese do not practice the primal religions from which these beliefs came, the traditions live on. Teachers, for obvious reasons, would not be advised to use such terms with their students.

In place of terms of endearment, ELD teachers can use a few everyday terms in Vietnamese students' L1 as a way to show them they are trying to learn the language and support home cultures. In Vietnamese, the word for "good morning" is *chào,* which is pronounced similar to the Italian word for goodbye, *ciao.* (Vietnamese is a tonal language, which means that vowels take on many more sounds than in Indo-European languages. Vietnamese was once written using an ideographic system of "characters" much as modern Chinese. However, when the French conquered Vietnam in the 1700s, they created a writing system that used the Roman alphabet, along with diacritical marks indicating the vowel tones. In the word

Think for a moment: What examples of code-switching have you heard inside the classroom? Outside the classroom? Have you ever tried it? If you don't recall hearing it, I challenge you to listen for it next time you are in a public place. There are multilingual people everywhere, and at least as many cell-phone users whose half-dialogues reach the ears of innocent bystanders every minute.

chào the "backward" accent mark tells us that the "a" is pronounced with a falling tone.)

TWO-WAY IMMERSION

For ELD teachers, especially those who work in elementary schools, two-way bilingual (sometimes called dual-language education) programs offer the chance to teach English in a program that fully promotes bilingualism. Although there are many forms that two-way programs can take (Lindholm-Leary 2001), the most common form requires that roughly half the students in a class be native speakers of one language, and one-half speak another common language. In the United States, Spanish-English two-way programs are by far the most common.

The attraction of two-way programs, irrespective of the supporting research, is clear. For bilingual education teachers who have seen their students—and themselves to a degree—attending parallel schools for many years, removed from "mainstream" students, two-way programs hold the promise of reintegration. In addition, many transitional bilingual teachers have longed for English-language "models" in the classroom. For ELD teachers who have watched as their native English-speaking students fail to learn even rudimentary Spanish, in spite of the nearby resources for learning the language, two-way instruction offers a way for these students to learn Spanish from native Spanish-speaking peers. An ELD teacher

in a two-way program may share two classes with a Spanish-speaking teacher. In the third grade, for instance, the
ELD teacher might teach science and social studies in English in the morning while her counterpart is teaching
mathematics and literacy in Spanish to the second class.
At midday, the classes switch. Participating students learn
content in two languages.

Although two-way programs appear to be the program on which we can all agree, a few commentators
have raised important questions about the motivation of
native English-speaking parents who want their children
to be bilingual. In fact, such parents are often active participants in the school culture and have the social capital
to promote and encourage two-way programs. Are such
families "using" native Spanish-speaking students so that
their children can learn a second language? Guadalupe
Valdés (1997) agrees with this assessment and further
speculates that the widespread success of two-way bilingual programs may eventually reduce employment opportunities for Latinos. She argues that when middle-
and upper-class whites speak Spanish, they will be given
the jobs that require bilingual skills. Such jobs are now
filled by Latinos.

Although the research on language learning in two-way
programs is impressive, in my opinion it suffers from a
sample bias not taken into consideration. I believe two-
way programs deserve praise more for their social aims
than for their academic gains. At least part of the motivation for the development of two-way programs grew from
a concern that transitional bilingual education unfairly
segregated students from each other. In some schools, for
instance, the bilingual and English-only classrooms had
little contact with one another, using entirely different
curricula and a set of teachers who never interacted.
Increasing contact among language groups in a single
school no doubt encourages positive social interactions.
As an evaluator of several two-way programs, I found that

they initiated social relationships never realized in a school where native Spanish speakers and English speakers had been separated in the same school for many years. For example, at L. A. Morgan Elementary in Galveston, Texas, we implemented a two-way (Spanish/English) program that avoided Valdés's concern about differential social capital among the families participating. At Morgan, the native English-speaking students are all African American and, like their Mexican American and Spanish-speaking counterparts, from the working class. As we implemented the program, the school saw, for the first time, many African American and Mexican American students becoming friends, inviting each other to birthday parties, sleepovers, and the like. Teachers at the school began to notice that families who had lived close by for years had started talking to one another, using the children as interpreters. And this all happened at a time when ethnic tensions in Galveston were strained.

In a particularly poignant story, one of the teachers overheard a Mexican American second-grade student telling his African American friend (in Spanish) that he would be afraid to go to high school, where he heard there were mean black students who beat up Mexican kids. His friend pointed out to him that he was black and that he was not mean and that he would never hurt him. Content with this explanation, they played together on the bars at every recess that day.

The challenge for ELD teachers is to create the kind of cultural mixing we saw at Morgan. The advantages of most, but certainly not all, two-way programs are social and cultural. In my view, learning the language is just the vehicle to the broader cultural benefits that come from two-way programs. Unfortunately, the sad fact is that schools and even school districts are becoming increasingly segregated (Orfield, Frankenberg, and Lee 2003), and thus the opportunities to create two-way programs are decreasing.

Think for a moment: Have you ever looked in the lunchroom at
your school (or possibly the one you attended as a student) and
seen that most of the students sorted themselves by gender,
ethnicity, and class? This is a common sight in schools across
America. What lesson could a non-dual-immersion school take from
these programs in an effort to desegregate in a natural, unforced
way?

CONCLUSION

Given a more complete picture of the role of native-
language instruction for ELL success, ELD teachers can
reflect thoughtfully on their role. Some ELD teachers
may decide that only bilingual education will do and
commit to learning the native language well enough to
provide instruction in that language. Others will make
certain that through the use of strategic code-switching
and cultural understanding, they will properly endorse
ELLs' home cultures or languages even if they do not
teach in the students' native languages. Still others may
choose to teach in a two-way program where their students will become bilingual and perhaps bicultural.
These are all worthy strategies in my view.

Nevertheless, a host of writers and researchers will
continue to argue that bilingual education is the only
possible language teaching option for ELLs, and ELD
teachers must be prepared to respond. In one of the more
widely read works on immigrant students in U.S. schools
(Olsen 1997), the author shares the story of a "new-
comer" high school, documenting the attitudes of the
school's teachers and administrators toward language education, whom she impugns: "There is little understanding [among the administrators and teachers] that when
primary language instruction is not provided to [ELL]
students, it means that they are being denied access to an

education. A student who speaks no English and is given instruction *only* in English is really being given no instruction at all" (101).

This statement might be an accurate description of the teachers and administrators' knowledge of language teaching at the school, but it is made without regard for a comprehensive view of expert ELD teaching, which we know can develop the self-efficacy and academic achievement of ELLs when it is done properly. If ELD teachers are to feel guilty about failing to engage in native-language instruction, such a sentiment can grow only from their own doubts and shortcomings as professional educators. Thoughtful, careful, and respectful teaching of English, in English, can result in empowered, academically enriched, and confident ELLs.

DISCUSSION QUESTIONS

1. Make a list of the benefits and drawbacks to each of the following school programs: ELD, bilingual education, dual immersion. Which kind of school would you feel most comfortable working in? Why? If you lived in a foreign country, which kind of school would you like to enroll your kids in? Why?

2. Discuss with another teacher: why is it important to validate students' home languages and cultures? List some ways you can do this in your classroom.

3. Refer back to Table 4.1 on different types of communication. Which are you most familiar with? Can you come up with a hypothetical example or explanation for each as it applies to you and your teaching?

4. For fun, look up some words in a language you are interested in and try code-switching with them with a friend. Perhaps you will inadvertently gain a new "fan" of that language!

FURTHER READING

Crawford, James. 1992. *Language Loyalties: A Source Book on the Official English Controversy.* Chicago: University of Chicago Press.
This widely read edited volume explores the complex relationship between our so-called common language and the political efforts to make it official. It is a bit dated, but contemporary readers will recognize the same, tired arguments made by those who do not appreciate the rich history of languages in the United States.

Parrish, Thomas, Maria Perez, Amy Merickel, and Robert Linquanti. 2006. "Effects of the Implementation of Proposition 227 on the Education of English Learners, K–12: Findings from a Five-Year Evaluation." San Francisco: American Institutes for Research.
This lengthy report is filled with interesting data. If you teach or plan to teach in California, or are just interested in the state's response to Proposition 227, then this report will be of interest.

Valdés, Guadalupe. 2001. *Learning and Not Learning English: Latino Students in American Schools.* New York: Teachers College Press.
My far more famous colleague Guadalupe Valdés's book follows four Latino middle-school ELLs. Poignant and heartbreaking, the book offers much for the ELD teacher to consider. Like all Valdés's works, it is superbly written.

CHAPTER FIVE

LANGUAGE TEACHING

Methods Less Familiar

- Conceptualizing L2 Learning Goals

- Making Music, Creating Language

- Objects and Images in ELD Classrooms

- The Importance of Images and Graphics in ELD

N HIS *LETTERS TO CRISTINA*, Paulo Freire recalls his early passion for language learning:

I have never forgotten the joy with which I welcomed exercises called "sentence forming" that our teacher gave us. She would ask me to write in a straight line all the words I knew. Afterward, I was supposed to form sentences with these words and later we discussed the meaning of each sentence I had created. This is how, little by little, I began to know my verbs, tenses, and moods; she taught me by increasing the level of difficulty. My teacher's fundamental preoccupation was not with making me memorize grammatical definitions but with stimulating the development of my oral and writing abilities. (Freire 1986, 29)

And so we learn that one of the most powerful contemporary writers on education learned his craft from a simple but elegant strategy, one that built clearly on what was known and a deep attention to meaning rather than rules.

Focus point

If there is one groove to be found on the road of language teaching in the past 150 years it is the move from trying to teach forms and rules to teaching language through ideas or content with a focus on communicative competence. For instance, from roughly 1850 to 1950, the dominant pedagogy in L2 instruction was the grammar-translation method. Educators who endorsed this technique believed that reading and writing were more important than oral language skills (listening and speaking), and that linking the target language to the native language through translation would encourage L2 competence. This method failed largely because students were asked to translate texts that they often did not understand well even in their native language. Even after months of translation exercises, students still had little command of the target language.

CONCEPTUALIZING L2 LEARNING GOALS

As we consider the role of instructional methods in L2 instruction, we ought to be clear about our goals. When we consider the content of language instruction for emerging ELLs, are we more interested in correct form (subject-verb agreement) or function (using the language in context even if some mistakes are made)? What do we want for the product of our instruction—an analysis of the lan-

---

Accuracy refers to the condition or quality of being true, correct, or exact; **fluency** is a speech and language pathology term that means the smoothness or flow with which sounds, syllables, words, and phrases are joined together when speaking quickly. **Language fluency** is used informally to broadly denote a high level of language proficiency, most typically a foreign language or another learned language.

guage or its use? Finally, with regard to the process or means for language, are we concerned primarily with accuracy or fluency?

In Figure 5.1 I have envisioned a perfect world of L1 acquisition, identified by its common features. I have also imagined a wholly imperfect world of L2 "teaching," with the word *teaching* in quotations because this is not representative of genuine teaching but rather its worst form. In this version of teaching, learners are subjected to learning language via dreary worksheets of decontextualized language drill in which correct form, rather than use, is the goal. Word definitions are memorized with no regard to their use in live language. Further, language teaching in this counterfeit world is conducted without regard for the ways that language is used to create social bonds. If we can agree that language learning is best achieved when it mirrors L1, then we should keep our

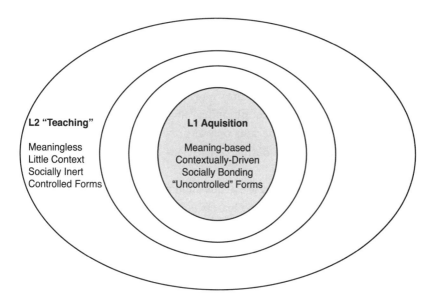

Figure 5.1 This figure shows the "core" of language teaching, one that is rooted in and seeks its inspiration from the principles of L1 acquisition. Far from the core or target of our instruction are the artificial forms of L2 teaching, where language form and dreary practice dominate.

aim there, and with each successive move away from this ideal, we must provide an increasingly better rationale for why we are using such methods. There may be a good reason why a teacher invites students to memorize words in isolation, but a sound reason is required. If we fail to consider the purpose and rationale for using overly "systematic" teaching forms, we are likely to be fooled into thinking that language teaching is like teaching skills, which it is most certainly not.

Methods such as the Natural Approach, which is based on Stephen Krashen's theory (discussed in Chapter 3), matches up well with contemporary notions of content-based instruction. As meaning in the target language became more important than controlling for syntax or lexicon, ELD teaching grounded in actual ob-

---

The Natural Approach is based on the following tenets:

- Language acquisition (an unconscious process developed through using language meaningfully) is different from language learning (consciously learning or discovering rules about a language), and language acquisition is the only way competence in a second language occurs (the acquisition/learning hypothesis).
- Conscious learning operates only as a monitor or editor that checks or repairs the output of what has been acquired (the monitor hypothesis).
- Grammatical structures are acquired in a predictable order, and it does little good to try to learn them in another order (the natural order hypothesis).
- People acquire language best from messages that are just slightly beyond their current competence (the input hypothesis).
- The learner's emotional state can act as a filter that impedes or blocks input necessary to acquisition (the affective filter hypothesis).

jects and events, where the focus was on the functional use of language in talking about whatever content was being presented, has become more commonplace.

Today we find the majority of ELD educators' pedagogy firmly rooted in a combination of the Natural Approach with a content-based focus. The instructional time of these educators is spent on a mixture of form and function tasks and activities, heavily weighted toward those activities that promote fluency (Li 2004). However, we should point out that disagreements regarding the role of form and function in L2 teaching remain. Research in this area has shown, not surprisingly, that the proper balance of form and function in language teaching depends largely on the goals of the language instruction.

I will share two methods that I believe are effective in ELL classrooms. Neither is particularly new or revolutionary—both are included in a well-known book on ELD methods (see Herrell and Jordon 2007). However, I have found that recent pressure for student achievement, particularly in U.S. schools, has diminished many teachers' ability or desire to use methods that do not appear, at least on the surface, to produce immediate measurable results in the way of language development. Requiring students to complete sentences using different adverbs, for instance, may *feel* as though we are helping them to gain accuracy and proper form in the target language, but research does not support such practices.

I hope to convince teachers and others that less "systematic" methods have both research and proven classroom success to support their use. For instance, playing music and singing in the ELD classroom may seem a bit uncomfortable at first, but it works remarkably well to promote language learning. Using objects in the classroom may be more difficult than simply having books and other texts in the classroom, but these methods are crucial, in my view, to promoting student engagement and language development.

Playing music and singing work remarkably well to promote language learning.

MAKING MUSIC, CREATING LANGUAGE

Focus point

The study of human language learning is confronted with great paradoxes in epistemology: How can we acquire language with such seeming ease, and then much later in life realize its immense complications upon further inspection? How can we study language using language? How can the world's languages appear to be so different and yet share so many common characteristics? It is this final question that drove me to consider the role of music in learning an L2.

In an article well worth reading, Marc Hauser and Josh McDermott (2003) point out that "throughout human history, on every part of the globe, in every extinct and extant culture, individuals have played and enjoyed music" (663). Because we can make the very same claim about language, anthropologists, neuroscientists, and linguists alike have tried to study the linkages between language and music. One obvious point of congruence is our ability to determine the grammaticality ("correctness") of a sentence and to point out when a melody contains a "sour" note. Both are learned without any direct instruction, appearing to be acquired by mere exposure to a particular dialect or musical scale. Another union joining music and language is the fact that although we can tell when an error has been made, we do not necessarily know which rule has been broken or even perhaps how to correct it. A native English speaker upon hearing the sentence "I want to see the new Cate Blanchett movie, that I've heard got great reviews," might recognize something as not quite right, in spite of having no idea why (hint: it has to do with essential versus nonessential clauses). Similarly, nearly all of us can tell if we hear an incorrect note on the major scale, but few know the properties of the incorrect note or perhaps even which note should have been played.

E. McMullen and J. R. Saffran (2004) suggest that the development of language and of music are not only similar but are in fact yoked to one another. Nearly every child becomes enchanted with music and rhyme at about age three, when they are also, not surprisingly, making great leaps in their capacity to communicate using language. In fact, I would argue that the child's fascination, even obsession, with music at this age suggests an essential stage of language development. And as many a stage theorist has argued, the stages of any cognitive development are invariant; that is, certain individuals might move through them at different rates, but all must eventually pass through. As teachers know, skipping a crucial stage often results in trouble down the line. It is just so with music, and L2 teachers must give music its due.

If we want language capacity to grow, we must develop musical skills, and vice versa. The research on this matter is clear: music aids language learning (Lowe 1998). Suzanne Medina (1990) found that music helped L2 learners learn the rhythm and diction of a new language. Kelleen Toohey and Elaine Day (1999) found that music "seduced" ELLs into language activities, encouraging participation by even the most reticent learners. A song written by a native English speaker using the melodic structure "native" to the target culture is imbued with important linguistic and phonological features. Rhythm and syntax are just two that come to mind.

Cross-Reference
For a related
discussion of
teaching
through the
arts, see Book 5,
Chapter 2.

At this point in the argument for using music in language-learning classrooms, most ELD teachers are convinced that music should play a part in their instruction. They mention that they are entirely willing to invite students to listen to and sing songs. My recommendation, however, goes a bit further, suggesting that teachers learn to play guitar and sing with their students, a proposal many find questionable if not downright crazy. The reasons to integrate music within an L2 program are clear, but many teachers ask—fairly—why it is important for them to learn to play the songs. Would not the same effect be achieved by playing the music from a prerecorded source and singing along to it? If the alternative is no music at all, then of course singing to prerecorded songs is preferred. But the act of taking a song and producing it together creates a kind of solidarity between teacher and students (and among students), which is nearly impossible to replicate any other way. The other primary purpose for playing the music live is that the teacher can alter the tempo of the music, among other features (e.g., lyrics, key). Recorded songs are often sung too quickly for L2 learners to make sense of the words. Live music can be modified to fit the needs of the learners.

Teachers may ask about the importance of playing a guitar in particular. Though it is true that other instruments can serve this purpose, a guitar (1) is transportable, (2) is fairly easy to learn, (3) is inexpensive, (4) allows one to sing and play at the same time (unlike wind instruments), and (5), has become perhaps the most recognized instrument in the world today.

So where does the initiated teacher begin? First, with a decent guitar, and by "decent" I mean one that stays roughly in tune, which will cost about $100–$150. A classical or steel string guitar will work fine. Buy a few lessons and an easy songbook (e.g., Snyder 1985) and you are ready to go. (Be sure to find a songbook designed for the guitar; many songbooks are designed for the piano and written in keys difficult to play on the guitar.)

Some Songs to Try in Your Classroom

The choice of songs is probably one of the least important decisions, but one easy guitar song to learn and sing with ELLs is the familiar "This Land Is Your Land" by Woody Guthrie, a song so thoughtfully constructed and lyrically charged it is hard to believe that you can play it using just three simple chords on the guitar. The song's lyrics not only have a wonderful repeating pattern that makes it easy for even beginning ELLs to join in, but the words also draw attention to the natural wonders and even social solidarity of the United States.

I saw above me an endless skyway
I saw below me a golden valley
This land was made for you and me

But later in the song, Guthrie names a few cultural icons and raises a question about that very solidarity.

In the squares of the city. In the shadow of the steeple
Near the relief office. I see my people
And some are grumblin' and some are wonderin'
If this land's still made for you and me.

One of the most compelling conversations I ever had with secondary ELLs came from discussing why Guthrie would include such a sad comment as "and some are wonderin' if this land's still made for you and me" in a song that begins by joyously extolling the beauty of the nation. We could not arrive at a satisfactory answer, but the conversation was rich.

If you are a confident musician, you might consider inviting your students to teach you a song in their native language. Depending on the age of your students, you might find a student in the class who is able to play that song on guitar, piano, or maybe accordion. It could be a great way to share culture in the classroom!

The thoughtful ELD teacher need not focus on folk songs alone, although the simpler chord structure of many such songs makes them easy to play. For instance, the traditional song "The Fox," recently made popular by the neo-bluegrass band Nickel Creek, is an excellent folk song to sing. Another great choice for ELD classrooms comes from the quirky Loudon Wainwright III, whose "The Swimming Song" offers ELLs a sample of everything lovely and inventive about the English language. A song perfectly suited to younger ELLs is commonly known as the Pizza Song. The call-and-response of the song requires no memorization, but the richness of the language makes it effective.

Teacher: "I am a pizza"—Students repeat each refrain,
e.g., "I am a pizza."
With extra cheese
From tomatoes
Sauce is squeezed
Onions and mushrooms
Oregano
Everyone sings the final refrain: "I am a pizza, ready to go"

The song continues with two or three more verses when we find that the pizza was dropped on the floor, a turn of the story that makes it even more fun.

The advantage of each of these songs is that they require no more than three guitar chords to play and can be played with a very simple downward strum, although various strumming and picking techniques can make them sound even better. Finding the chords to thousands of songs these days is as simple as searching on the Internet for the name of the song and the word "chords." My search using "The Swimming Song" and "chords" turned up several Web pages with the lyrics and guitar chords.

Experienced ELD teachers may be familiar with many different language-teaching programs that use chants and other rhythmic patterns to teach language. In one particularly popular program, whose name I will not mention, the promotion of "songs" in the ELD classroom is stilted and oddly metered sentences designed to teach syntactical patterns. They are not poems or songs. They are instead so contrived that no teacher or student would be compelled to sing them. Needless to say, I do not endorse this less authentic, less fun, and less musical form of language teaching.

The Magic of Rhymes and Songs

In a wonderful quote from Susan Ohanian (see Weaver 1988) she shares a story about how she noticed that her low readers (native English speakers) were unable to

catch on to rhyming patterns presented as decontextualized word pairs (e.g., cat-mat), but when she read books
with rhyming patterns, they caught on with ease. She
further noticed that as they learned to rhyme, they also
learned to read. My wife, Sarah, an elementary teacher
herself, who has been exposed to her share of reading
theories and implemented many complicated reading
programs, remains convinced that reading *Hop on Pop* by
Dr. Seuss remains the most reliable strategy for teaching
children to read. In her view, you need just this one
book, read over and over, discussed for its moral impera-
tives ("What's wrong with jumping on your dad or
mom?") and just plain silliness, to jumpstart the reading
process.

For reasons that are likely hidden in the mysteries of our
minds and language itself, rhyming patterns, like songs, coax
the flux of arbitrary sounds and symbols into coherency. In
addition to helping to organize meaning, songs and rhymes
reveal the playful nature of language, something that I do
not believe classrooms can go without.

Focus point

OBJECTS AND IMAGES IN ELD CLASSROOMS

Although the debate is largely outside of the conversations of teachers, researchers in psychology, anthropology, and other fields have created a dualism between
what is called "formal" learning (i.e., learning in schools)
and "informal" learning (i.e., learning in homes, communities, or museums). A key article in this tradition
seems to argue that formal schooling actually reduces a
child's capacity for logical and divergent thinking (Scribner and Cole 1973). More recent writers in this area have
suggested that learning outside of school is more genuine, long-lasting, and enjoyable. I agree somewhat with
this argument, but I would also point out that most of
the researchers in this tradition are not teachers, and
some seem to delight in providing yet another round of
criticism of schools.

Teachers, for their part, understand clearly that the classroom cannot provide as rich an environment for learning of, say, a comprehensive museum of science, but will quickly counter with the fact that well-designed and sufficiently integrated field trips provide students with opportunities to engage in "informal" learning opportunities. Teacher also are willing to agree that classrooms are not necessarily the places most conducive to learning, but plenty of genuine learning can happen there under the guidance of an expert educator.

If we press our L1/L2 analogy once more, creating L1 conditions in school would mean bringing more of the outside world into the classroom. First-language learning clearly relies on the use of immediate objects for lexical development. How could a child learn to name things if no "things" existed? It therefore stands to reason that L2 development, which requires learners to develop a new lexicon, would benefit from objects in the learning environment. *Unlike arguing for a false dualism between formal and informal learning, making the ELD classroom more like the outside world is a proposal worthy of discussion.* Bringing the objects of learning (not just their representations in text or images) into the classroom serves two functions: making the classroom a more genuine learning experience for all students, and helping ELLs to acquire/learn language rapidly. We know that real objects are crucial for L1 learning; uncovering the reasons *why* is important if we are to address their importance in L2.

Focus point

Think for a moment: Where/when/how can informal learning occur on your school grounds? Are there ways to promote this kind of learning more often than, say, budgets, permission slips, and school buses would allow? What venue for informal learning do you wish you had more time, money, or other resources for or access to? Why?

The philosopher Willard Quine (1960) makes object naming the centerpiece of his work, aptly titled *Word and Object*, a book considered a milestone in the philosophy of language. His most compelling example of the challenge of learning and studying the acquisition of the meaning of words, and the example most relevant to the present discussion, concerns a traveler who embarks on a journey with a member of an entirely unfamiliar culture, whose language the traveler is learning. When a rabbit comes into view, the guide points to it and says *gavagai*. The problem for the traveler is to understand how the stimulus object, the rabbit, relates to the sound symbol *gavagai*. Quine points out that the traveler's first assumption may be that *gavagai* maps directly to the term *rabbit* in his native English. But this is certainly not the only possible meaning. For instance, the culture could rely on rabbits for food, and thus *gavagai* could be a mass term, used to refer to all animals that are eaten. From this possibility Quine moves into territory that speaks to his training as a philosopher of language, suggesting that the traveler might interpret *gavagai* as "undetached" rabbit parts. An entirely different term might be used when considering a rabbit cut up and ready for cooking. Quine's story has been used repeatedly to illustrate how speakers of two different languages might differ so widely on meaning that it could be impossible for anyone to learn another's language.

My primary point in sharing Quine's translation problem is that even when objects are used as teaching aids, what is learned cannot be determined for certain. It

Think for a moment: What else could *gavagai* mean in this context? What if it were a verb, a phrase, or even a pronoun? Work with a friend and make a long and creative list. Then consider how your ELLs might possibly misinterpret you when you point to an object and say a word.

seems quite possible that a learner would confuse the names for objects other than what the language intends. Yet we find few instances of Quine's dilemma in L2 teaching. Students seem to easily grasp the limits and markers of the object at hand, learning terms quite easily without the troubles Quine pondered.

Why is it that the terms for objects in the environment are not more commonly confusing? The answer comes from research on L1 acquisition. It appears that the more dramatic and circumscribed (or "foregrounded") the object, the more likely it will be for the L2 learner to create a reliable relation between object and word. The linguist Eve Clark (1995) hypothesized that early word learning in L1 was based on the physical features of the object itself. To prove her point, Clark used parent journals to corroborate the common view that *doggy* or *kitty* was as likely as *mommy* to be a child's first word. Her research told us why. The work of Clark and others shows that the following objects appear to be easily learned during L1 acquisition: (1) animated objects, (2) objects unique in the local environment (e.g., objects that move), (3) objects that fit into a learner's vision field (i.e., a large building would be unlikely to be an early term), and (4) objects with features that interact with the learner's several sensory systems. It appears these principles hold for L2 learning as well.

Key concept
realia

In the L2 field, the term used for objects in teaching is *realia*. And whereas the rationale for L2 seems clear, the-

ELD teachers and researchers have their own argot, or specialized code words, and the term *realia* is a good example of such specialization. Realia is commonly understood as the objects made available to ELLs that connect to the language and content objectives in the classroom. The term also describes the artifacts of the customs and traditions of a specific culture, also key to helping L2 learners gain proficiency.

ories on the use of realia unique to L2 instruction are rare.

However, the lack of a well-developed theory has not prevented ELD teachers from recognizing their importance. Following is a typical example in the L2 literature, taken from a popular book of teaching methods in beginning L2 instruction: "If language learning truly involves meaningful communication and reflection, often about concrete and mutual referents, then it is crucial that you have all kinds of different enticing objects for display and use in your classroom, and ones that appeal to all the senses" (Enright and McCloskey 1988, 111).

This statement reveals the taken-for-granted importance of objects in the language-learning classroom. Realia helps to make English-language input as comprehensible as possible and to build connections between the classroom and the world (e.g., Zukowski-Faust 1997). Realia in a classroom can lead to activities such as role-playing, acting, and use of the whole body in demonstration of the objects' actions or use. What realia do you have in your classroom, and how could you use it more often in your lessons? In a recent study, M. W. Roney (1994) shares how a Spanish-language teacher uses an ornate dollhouse in the classroom to teach family names, relationships, and prepositions such as *outside* and *inside*.

Using Objects in Teaching

Given the importance and necessity of using objects in the classroom, teachers should do all they can to introduce objects in the classroom and have them available for students. ELD teachers can comb garage sales and thrift stores, seeking out every opportunity to use objects for teaching. Other resources might be available for borrowing objects for teaching in the classroom. For instance, many local museums have loan or checkout programs for "experience boxes," which contain compelling instructional

Focus point

objects. One of the nation's best loan programs is the
Harris Educational Loan Center, part of the Field Museum in Chicago. The collection holds one of my favorite examples of experience boxes. Titled "Fishing in
the Americas," the box holds replicas of fishing tools and
techniques used by past and present indigenous peoples
of the Americas. The box brings to life the creativity of
past cultures' quests for food found in the rivers, lakes,
and seas. This set of realia can be used in concert with
modern fishing tools, easily found at any sporting goods
store. ELLs can then share in writing their own fishing
experiences, in which they might be encouraged to tell a
"fish story." In addition, a visit to an ocean pier or lake
near an urban area may reveal a wide range of immigrants trying their luck at fishing. Fishing from shore or
pier is an inexpensive way to spend leisure time, and it
sometimes provides food for lower-income families;
thus, we find that a curricular focus on fishing might
connect particularly well to our ELL students' lives.

Another example of useful objects for L2 instruction
comes from a recent chapter on the role of realia in the
teaching of science to ELLs (Ash, Téllez, and Crain
2009), which suggests that ELD teachers can create engaging learning stations by using easy-to-find animals.
For instance, garden snails offer students an excellent
way to talk about animal movement. Students can record
the travels of several snails in a simple terrarium. Small
marks on the snails' shells help them to keep track; their
slow movement allows for intermittent recording and
discussion. Combined with other curricular materials

Consider what other activities your students might be familiar with
outside of class, such as sports. What kinds of realia could you bring
to class to help engage students in conversation? Where could you
get these items inexpensively (or better yet, free)?

and connections to fictional works, snails provide a useful "object" for science study for ELLs.

Another advantage of realia is that they can help ELLs to better understand their new culture. In a manner similar to the way an anthropologist might use artifacts to understand a culture, immigrant ELLs can be asked to consider the ways that realia explain life in a new country. For instance, a fast-food hamburger as a cultural object has no peer for a teacher trying to help immigrant learners make sense of what is both good and bad about life in the United States (see Shor 1987).

On a final note, it might seem that by suggesting we use objects for word learning in L2 classrooms, I am contradicting my earlier suggestion for learning the meanings of words in sentences rather than in isolation. This is a fair question, but in practice, it is impossible to share an object in the classroom without using sentences and genuine language. Realia in the classroom do not encourage a simple single meaning between word and object.

THE IMPORTANCE OF IMAGES AND GRAPHICS IN ELD

Realia have a specific advantage for ELD and L2 teaching, but some objects simply cannot be transformed into classroom realia. Whales, submarines, and pyramids, for instance, must be represented to ELLs in some other manner. When the curriculum turns to these topics, images, both moving and still, provide the extralinguistic support needed for ELD instruction, and the research has demonstrated clearly the cognitive advantages of learning with both words and pictures.

Instructional practices that build on this linkage include the use of graphic organizers, juxtaposed text and images, multi- and hypermedia, film, and objects. A graphic organizer is an instructional tool used to illustrate or pictorially represent relationships among objects or ideas. Flowcharts and food webs are examples of graphic organizers; see Google for more examples. While not working from the tradition of second-language education, Edward Tufte (1990), whose work has become popular among cognitive theorists who study comprehension of scientific concepts, helps us to understand the valuable role visual images can play in learning when he writes, "Visual displays of information encourage a diversity of individual viewer styles and rates of editing, personalizing, reasoning, and understanding. Unlike speech, visual displays are simultaneously a wide-band and a perceiver-controllable channel" (31).

Tufte's point is particularly important for ELLs. Rate of delivery, comprehensible input, and self-regulated attention are key factors in helping ELLs understand what is being said. Similarly, a page of written text, without any visual representation, can be a daunting challenge for any ELLs. This is why graphic organizers are so crucial for language and content learners. Most teachers are familiar with the use of graphic organizers. Venn diagrams, semantic webs, and other representations should be familiar, but I think it is important for teachers to consider the need for such tools and perhaps go beyond the traditional graphic tools, stretching into photo annotations and other creative ways of representing knowledge.

In general studies of learning, the theoretical rationale for combining words and images as aids to comprehension has come largely from multimedia learning. Researchers in this area have found, for instance, that struggling secondary school ELLs engaged in "coping" strategies that included the use of visual aids to comprehension, even when the instruction failed to (or perhaps discouraged) the use of images as a tool to aid language learning.

For ELD teachers, using images for instruction has never been easier. First, the Internet is a boon. Its capacity for storing and making images easily available continues to grow. Digital cameras, scanners, and video cameras can be purchased very cheaply, allowing teachers to create their own curricula embedded with images deeply connected to the language of their lessons. One good example from my own experience comes from a project at a two-way bilingual school in California. After receiving a small grant, the school purchased two digital video recorders and several computers with movie editing software built in. (All Apple Macintosh computers come with iMovie, an easy way to access a movie editing software package.) During a unit on birds, the fourth-grade class took a field trip to a nature preserve and took videos of the birds they found there. Upon return to school, their task was to provide a "voice-over" of the video identifying the type of bird and its habitat, as well as other information. The videos were then shared with younger students, who would be going to the same preserve the following year. Those students, in turn, created their own video, adding new birds and additional information while also using some footage from the previous class' efforts. Asking ELLs to teach other students seems to be a very good way to encourage authentic language use as well as providing a purpose for their work. It would perhaps be a challenge to think of an object whose image *cannot* be found using Google or any other search engine. Using video and camera equipment in a classroom to create your own images is in some ways analogous to a class that makes its own music, complete with guitar playing and singing, as opposed to listening to or watching prerecorded song. The prerecorded images and music are good, but they are not the best representation for engaging students in language learning.

This teacher-directed example of multimedia learning provides a good opportunity to consider the value of commercially produced instructional software for language learning. Although there are several popular language-teaching programs, ELD teaching is largely about meeting the needs of students through customized curriculum, which commercial programs cannot do. Specifically, teacher-led technology can be tailored to students' specific instructional needs and connected with the content of instruction, as in the aforementioned bird study example. Thus, although it might be tempting to think that we can take our students to a computer lab, run the software, and realize great gains in language instruction, the research does not bear out this promise. With even marginal technology skills, teachers can use images and audio that technology provides to easily combine words, images, and graphics into a compelling curriculum for ELLs. Such integrated instruction has proven very beneficial.

> Think for a moment: Most administrators encourage their teachers to employ technology in the classroom. Have you ever felt pressured to use a computer lab that didn't clearly benefit students in their language goals? How might you present a more productive use of technology in your curriculum? Could you use some of the ideas presented in this chapter?

CONCLUSION

In this chapter, we have explored how L2 learning can be made similar to L1 learning. Music as a vehicle for language acquisition appears to capitalize on connections between the development of musical knowledge and language. I therefore argue that music must be a part of any language-learning classroom and suggest that teachers should learn to play live music with their students. Objects and talk about them are also essential features of L1 and have a definite role to play in the L2 classroom. Teachers can leverage many resources for using objects, or realia, in the average classroom that will mimic the world of exploration found in L1. Finally, images and other graphic tools are crucial in the L2 classroom. With minimal technology skills, teachers can create dynamic multimedia instructional materials.

DISCUSSION QUESTIONS

1. To help you organize your own thoughts about strategies you can employ to assist in content area language teaching, fill in the following table (you may need to do this on a separate sheet of paper so that you have sufficient space). Suggestion: share this table with your department.

	Realia	Music	Organizers	Image/Video	Poetry/Rhymes
Math					
Science					
Social Studies					
English					
Health					

2. Which of the methods you filled in on the table are most challenging to you? Who can help you to implement them?

3. Imagine how you would explain to a parent the benefits of realia, music, graphic organizers, image, video, and poetry in language learning. Can you justify their use?

FURTHER READING

Shor, Ira. 1983. *Critical Teaching and Everyday Life*. South Handley, MA: Bergin and Garvey.
Shor's work is often overlooked in the field of critical pedagogy, yet I believe he might be paradoxically more sophisticated and practically minded than his contemporaries. In this book he demonstrates how to use cultural objects in critical teaching. He is not necessarily an ELD teacher, but many of his students are working-class. By "deconstructing" objects, he helps them to learn the roots of power and privilege.
Storr, Anthony. 1993. *Music and the Mind*. New York: Ballantine.
Storr (1920–2001) was a psychotherapist who took on the task of explaining why music is part of all human culture. Although I find parts of his

argument dubious, the range of evidence he presents will be of interest to any teacher who has noticed the power of music in children and youth.

Tufte, Edward. 1990. *Envisioning Information.* Cheshire, CT: Graphics Press. Tufte shows us the power of visual thinking. Teachers who are curricular designers will learn much from Tufte's explorations.

- Attachment in the ELD Classroom
- Language and Attachment Theory
- The Emotional Side to L2 Development
- Two Kinds of Language Learners

CHAPTER SIX

THE ELD TEACHER

A Special Psychology

ALL THOUGHTFUL AND CARING teachers have a psychological pull toward their students. We want our students to learn from us, even to enjoy our instruction, but we know that our relationships are, by design, short-lived. We try to balance our desire to care for our students with the knowledge that they must learn to do things for themselves and that teaching is at heart about creating independent learners. As Anna Freud, the daughter of Sigmund Freud and a noted psychoanalyst herself, once said, "A mother's job is to be there [and then] to be left" (quoted in Furman 1982, 15). Those readers who are mothers themselves may not appreciate this point of view, but it is absolutely true that caregivers who foster a healthy, independent child, one who views her accomplishments as her own and who is not afraid of facing the wider world, have done their job well.

The same is true of teachers, but we tend not to bristle at the phrase when it is applied directly to educators: "A teacher's job is to be there and then to be left." It sounds less threatening. After all, we should more or less expect

All thoughtful and caring teachers have a psychological pull toward their students.

Focus point

that teachers will work toward their own irrelevancy. Students must learn to do for themselves those tasks and skills they once needed a teacher's help to do. Much as Vygotsky's zone of proximal development suggests (Vygotsky 1978), the whole enterprise of learning is the movement from doing activities and creating thoughts on one's own that once needed a more capable partner.

But what of the intersection between the role of a caregiver and the teacher? Teachers are not parents, and parents are not teachers, at least not in the formal sense. What implications might we find when teachers are helping students learn a new language, the language of the wider community in which the immigrant family is now a part of? What are the psychological implications when a teacher is now in the role of language teacher and teaching the language that will provide the student access to the wide world? Can the same L1 emotional bonds hold when students are learning L2?

ATTACHMENT IN THE ELD CLASSROOM

Some years ago I was working with a high school teacher in Orange County, California, who had recently begun teaching ELD after several years as a social studies teacher for native English speakers. As part of the school-university collaborative, we were searching for ways to modify the existing social studies curriculum to better meet the needs of her ELLs. I cannot recall exactly the native languages of the students, but I do remember a mix of Spanish, Vietnamese, Russian, and Arabic speakers. Their educational backgrounds were equally varied. About half had received extensive schooling in their home countries; some of the parents had earned bachelor's degrees whereas other parents had not completed the sixth grade. One day after her classes had ended, the teacher shared with me a characteristic of her ELLs that was at once appealing and exasperating: "I've never worked with high school students who became so attached to me. They come into my class during breaks, at lunch, and sometimes after school. Sometimes I have to tell them that I need a break, just to grade papers or eat my lunch in peace. They are really good kids, and I do like talking to them, but I can't seem to figure out why they are always in my room. Native English-speaking students never did this."

As the school year progressed, the ELLs seemed to need the teacher less, but she remained intrigued by the attention she received from them. As we talked more about her predicament, we reasoned that her classroom was the one place where the English language was adapted to the ELLs' needs. This was the place where errors in English were not met with puzzled looks or derision but with a kindly restatement using the correct form or term. Perhaps it was also the only context where they could safely talk to one another using the beginning English "dialect" they all spoke. In addition, the teacher had a warm and caring demeanor and had herself come to the United States from the Philippines as a teenager, giving her an opportunity to share her own experiences.

In my work with ELD teachers before and since, a great many have described a similar experience, regardless of the age of the students. Having noticed a similar phenomenon with my own ELL students, I decided to investigate possible explanations.

If we agree that some of the processes for L1 acquisition are similar for L2 acquisition, then it should not surprise us that the psychological processes at work between learner and language model might also be alike. Learning an L1 in an emotionally healthy context means that a

---

In your own experience as an ELD instructor, have your students been attached to you in the way described here? If so, do the reasons given hold true in your experience? What other reasons might your students have for hanging out in your classroom (or not)?

child's primary caregiver not only shares language but also shares an intense emotional bond that is never fully repeated. The same, but less intense, psychological processes may be at work when an ELD teacher becomes the person most responsible for teaching a student a new language. This became a working theory of mine and the guiding principle for the investigation I present here.

This chapter may at times seem more psychological than pedagogical, but it is my view that the two can never fully be separated, especially when considering ELLs. Why might this be the case? If we begin by considering that a child's primary caregiver is the person who provides both the most explicit language model and the most psychological nurturing, then it seems logical to conclude that ELLs form more intense attachments with their language teachers than do other students. After all, they are dependent on their teacher for making their new world comprehensible.

LANGUAGE AND ATTACHMENT THEORY

The theme of attachment seems to arise regularly when considering the relationship between ELLs and their teachers. This is a convenient theme to begin our considerations because it has been investigated extensively in the developmental and analytic psychology literature. The work of John Bowlby is central to our understanding of attachment in the young infant (Bowlby 1982; 1999). His primary contribution, known as *attachment theory*, suggests that infants need at least one clear and responsive caregiver in order for healthy psychological development. Bowlby further explicated his theory by demonstrating that certain attachment failures result in specific psychological troubles later in one's life (although we will not be considering his thoughts on pathology). His theory even proposed that our species holds various instinctual patterns that drive us toward healthy attachment processes.

Key concept
attachment
theory

Attachment theory seems at first glance an unlikely application for ELD teaching, or any teaching for that matter. The ELLs who attend school are not infants. And though we cannot be certain that each student has had a healthy attachment, the process would appear to be over by the time school attendance begins. Even the youngest ELLs in schools are four to five years old, well beyond infancy or toddler age. However, one very interesting study demonstrated that a caregiver's language adaptations for the developing infant and toddler are central to the attachment process (Holzman 1984). This work suggests that the contours of a caregiver's reactions to infant vocalizations play a primary role in the attachment process. If this is indeed the case, then we might generalize to ELLs in a school context, and understand that they might be forming emotional attachments beyond the "regular" bonds shared by a teacher and his or her students. We might further be convinced of this special relationship if we agree with Bowlby and others who suggest that the attachment process is instinctual (e.g., Ainsworth 1969).

At one extreme, we might believe that ELD teachers who want to develop psychologically healthy language learners should form strong emotional attachments, in a way mimicking an infant's caregiver. But such an extreme position would ignore a fundamental part of attachment theory. Although Bowlby argued that a consistent emotional attachment was necessary for healthy emotional growth, the caregiver who fails to allow the infant independent exploration creates too great an attachment, which has its own negative consequences. The most effective strategy is creating a balance between providing a safe psychological "home base" and encouraging an independent and confident individual.

Another related theory of attachment comes from Margaret Mahler, whose psychoanalytic perspective has informed our understanding of infant, toddler, and adolescent development (Mahler, Pine, and Bergman 2000).

Mahler's fundamental theory, known as Separation-Individuation, refers to the development of the differentiation between the child and the caregiver and of the child's own identity, which she and her colleagues argue includes language development and cognitive abilities.

Through careful research, Mahler noticed that well-adjusted youth had experienced a successful separation from their primary caregiver, which resulted in a healthy sense of self, or individuation. Specifically, within a period she called *rapprochement* (which happens at about age two to three), psychologically healthy children experience a balance of consistent caregiver attention and encouragement to explore the world on their own. An example of how rapprochement works in the healthy child/caregiver relationship was shared with me by one of my graduate instructors, Jonathan Brower. He pointed out that two-year-olds want to explore the world, find interesting things, and bring them back to show their caregiver, providing evidence of their burgeoning independence. These seemingly small events, crucial in the development of the child's individuation, can be seen right now, firsthand, at any park, in any city around the world. A two-year-old leaves the close psychological space of her father and ventures a safe distance from him, finds a tiny but harmless insect, and brings it back. The father's reaction has everything to do with how this child will experience her individuation.

In most instances, the father will be engaged in the activity, recognize the child's effort, and begin a conversation ("Look at the bug's feet . . . See how it crawls . . . Let's be sure to put it back where you found it," and so on). This simple interchange has encouraged the child to explore the world independently, engage in an individual effort, and then share the initial phase of the bug-finding experience, for which the father was not present, using language. Duplicate this experience many times over, and Mahler would argue that the result is a psychologically healthy child. In fact, Mahler termed a successful rapprochement as the "psychological birth" of the child.

Now imagine how this process might go wrong. First, imagine that the child has no stable caregiver from whom to separate. This condition leads to very serious separation issues later in life. Second, imagine that the father is so overly cautious that he never allows his daughter to do anything independently. Again, here is a choice that discourages healthy separation. Third, imagine that he chides her for bringing him a "dirty" insect. Or imagine that he ignores her efforts and says nothing. Mahler and her colleagues discovered that a child's *rapprochement* plays out repeatedly into childhood and young adulthood. *Adolescents whose rapprochement is unresolved lack a strong sense of self and may turn to unhealthy ways of coping with their new identities.*

Focus point

THE EMOTIONAL SIDE TO L2 DEVELOPMENT

How might separation and individuation be related to L2 development? At the intersection of language and attachment, it appears that primary caregivers who foster healthy emotional growth understand not only the importance of physical proximity for their infant but also the role of linguistic "safety" and experimentation in development. They know, probably instinctively, when to repeat or rephrase a toddler's speech, when to infer and then state what the child is thinking, and when to encourage the child to speak on her own. One feature of attachment theory that relates well to ELD teaching is the notion that infants require a consistent caregiver who not only is both physically and psychologically available but also encourages the infant to explore the world independently.

Our understanding of attachment can help to explain why the Orange County teacher's ELLs stayed in her room at lunchtime, wanted the safety of her class, and, at least early in the year, appeared fearful of the wider world of the school. Of course, the teacher did not discourage the students' dependency on her, nor did she allow them to stay in her room at every break. When the time came—and only she knew when that time was right— she had to encourage them to interact with other students and teachers in the school, "pushing the chicks from the nest," to borrow a metaphor.

What I noticed early on as an ELD teacher is that some of the L2 theories and strategies I learned seemed very related to the idea of psychological attachment and rapprochement. It is worth exploring and connecting some of these psychological theories with those that are familiar to L2 teachers. In fact, given the psychological nature of L2 learning, it is not surprising that ELD teachers and researchers have developed methods that leverage the relationship between students and teachers. One of the more compelling examples of a "humanistic" method of L2 teaching is known as community language learning (CLL), developed in the 1960s by a priest and therapist named Charles A. Curran (1983).

The fundamental belief behind Curran's pedagogy is that learning a new language makes us confront an existential anxiety. Like all teaching/learning relationships, emotional issues emerge, and teachers can either address them thoughtfully or ignore them at their peril. As described by Karin Ryding, one of Curran's best interpreters (see Ryding 1993), CLL has forced language teachers to confront issues of trust, the use of silence in the classroom, the importance of feelings and affirmation in language teaching, and the stages of psychological growth. None of these had previously been considered important in L2 settings. Ryding suggests that CLL has drawn great interest but few practitioners. I agree that few L2 teachers identify with CLL as an approach, but no teacher fully escapes the psychological tensions described in CLL. Jean-Marc Dewaele (2005) suggests that L2 researchers and educators have ignored the role of emotional development in the learning of languages: "Language teachers need to be aware that cultural/typological distance between the learners' L1(s) and their L2 is an important obstacle in mastery of emotional speech" (8).

In my view, the professional L2 teacher must know, at the very least, the stages of learner growth that Curran described and recognize whether he or she is creating teacher dependency or a healthy independence among learners.

Curran described the sequence as follows:

1. "Birth" stage: feelings of security and belonging are established.

2. As the learners' ability improves, they achieve a measure of independence from the parent.

3. Learners can speak independently.

4. The learner is secure enough to take criticism and being corrected.

5. The learner becomes an "adult" speaker and a "knower."

In this list we see the importance of creating independent learners and find clear connections to infant and early child development theories discussed earlier.

It is a mistake, however, to think that teachers should treat their students as young children, but the developmental stages for students learning a new language put them clearly in a psychological state that resembles the child's predicament. Curran himself recognized the commonalities: "Learning, then, as we can see in this switch

Think for a moment: How can you apply Curran's stages to your L2 learners? Can you come up with some descriptions and examples (hypothetical or real) that fit each stage?

from knower superiority (in one's native language) to submissive inferiority (in the target language), involves the learner in a temporary psychological return to the state of a small child with its concomitant sense of weakness, anxiety, inadequacy, and dependency" (Curran 1983, 169). Even when we are working with adult L2 learners, we find students facing great self-doubt, as well as a new and perhaps discomforting reliance on the teacher. In a very compelling paper, Y. Cohen and Marlene Norst (1989) share the learning journals of adults— all graduate students and monolingual speakers—who are learning a second language. One journal entry is particularly interesting: "What have I learnt? I think more about myself than (L2). My relationship and respect for the teacher seems paramount in facilitating my learning. I need positive encouragement, something which [the teacher] gave me and made me regain confidence in myself" (71). Cohen and Norst further suggest that second-language learning places new and challenging demands on learners with respect to self-representation. Essentially, they maintain that to learn a second language is to take on a new identity (Guiora et al. 1972).

TWO KINDS OF LANGUAGE LEARNERS

In my view, the world of all L2 learners can be divided into two groups. The first group (by far the smaller of the two) sees language as a puzzle to be solved. For them, learning a new language is about the intricacies of the rules and patterns (both phonological and semantic) and fitting them together correctly, especially in the written form. Accuracy and analysis are paramount to these learners. I believe that many foreign-language teachers belong to this group, and many of them teach languages in the analytical, puzzle-style manner they favor. The second group consists of error-making, meaning-focused talkers who want to *use* the language to communicate. We want to get it right, but we mostly want to understand and be

> Think for a moment: What kind of language learner are you, a puzzle-solver or a communicator? Have you taught both kinds of language-learning students? If so, how did you tailor instruction to meet their individual needs?

understood, in the same way we wanted to be heard and listened to when we acquired our first language. If we make a mistake, we do not necessarily want to be told about which rule we broke or ignored, as long as we are understood. We are nervous learners, insecure and often afraid to enter the world of native speakers for fear we will not understand, be misunderstood, or both.

Given the highly psychological nature of L2 learning, ELD teachers must be constantly on the lookout for students who are connecting to them in ways that do not encourage independence. Like the teacher described earlier, they must move their students from the safe and secure language classroom—where mistakes are allowed and even encouraged at times, no one laughs at your "accent," and you have the right to just listen if you do not have the words—into the great, wide world of native speakers, who do not generally slow down, who might ask you "Where are you from?" and who will wait only so long for a response.

Practically, we must be fully aware of those students who need extra encouragement to try their skills among native speakers and those who need to slow down a bit in their zeal to use their new language. We must do our part to protect immigrant students from the perils found in contemporary U.S. society while not discouraging them from forming relationships with other students, all the while recognizing the stages of each ELL's psychological development.

We must also recognize the value of forming strong emotional ties among learners. *Teachers generally do not follow students throughout their academic lives, but the*

Focus point

students themselves often stay with one another. It is there-
fore a wise decision for us to help create strong bonds among
our students. The building of strong relationships among
students does not carry the disadvantages of overreliance
on a teacher. Zoltan Dörnyei and Angi Malderez (1999)
suggest several ways in which language teachers can foster healthy affiliations among their students:

1. Proximity—Chances to be near one another in
   learning tasks.

2. Interaction—Learning opportunities in which the
   behavior of each person influences other group
   members.

3. Cooperation—Conditions in which students
   must strive for mutual benefit.

4. Successful completion of whole group tasks—
   these build a sense of group achievement.

5. Intergroup competition—Careful and probably
   limited use of activities such as games in which
   groups of students work together against other
   groups.

6. Joint hardships—Provides a special case of group
   achievement, in which members are drawn together by enduring a difficult situation.

7. Common threat—Students form solidarity when
   facing, for instance, a big project or examination.

We might recognize in these strategies connections to cooperative learning, which I will not explore in depth because the methods are very well-known and explored
fully in many resources. Creating solidarity among language learners may be more critical than cooperative
learning, owing to the nature of their unique psychological development.

CONCLUSION

I believe that ELD teachers tend to form stronger relationships with their students than do other teachers. This chapter explored this phenomenon with an eye toward helping teachers understand more about their crucial role in helping immigrant students negotiate their new world. When L1 learning is compared with L2 learning, the comparison draws important similarities between teaching and parenting. Attending to the nuances of ELLs' psychological growth as language learners may lead some to rethink ELD teaching as a career too complicated for anyone. That is not my intent, nor do I believe that teachers must be trained as therapists. I want only for teachers to be aware of the psychological processes that will unfold in their classrooms, whether they wish them to or not. If teachers are aware of the particular bonding and attachment that often accompany L2 learners, as well as students' specific needs to experiment in safe settings, their students will be better able to grow into thoughtful, healthy, independent learners.

DISCUSSION QUESTIONS

1. What are the implications of the special relationship between teacher and language learners?

2. Consider what a student might be like if he is an adolescent whose rapprochement is unresolved, he lacks a strong sense of self, or he turns to unhealthy ways of coping with his new identity. How could you help him to learn an L2 as well as come to terms with his identity? Or is it too late?

3. How can a teacher effectively "push the chicks out of the nest" as the end of a school year nears? What are ways to foster independence without creating hurt feelings or rejection?

FURTHER READING

Arnold, Jane, ed. 1999. *Affect in Language Learning*. Cambridge: Cambridge University Press.

This edited volume is an excellent resource for language teachers interested in the role of emotion in language learning. Individual chapters address several techniques of L2 teaching, including the often-misunderstood Suggestopedia.

Dörnyei, Zoltan. 2005. *The Psychology of the Language Learner: Individual Differences in Second Language Acquisition*. Mahwah, NJ: Lawrence Erlbaum.

Dörnyei explores the concept of individual differences as operationalized definitions, focusing clearly on how we measure constructs such as motivation. The book can be tedious for those who do not hold a deep interest in assessment, but it should be required reading for all educators who use the term *learning styles* without any research basis.

Mahler, Margaret S., Fred Pine, and Anni Bergman. 2000. *The Psychological Birth of the Human Infant: Symbiosis and Individuation*. New York: Basic Books.

For those who are interested in the psychological processes of individuation, I would highly recommend this book. It will help both parents and adult children understand why some achievements are satisfying and others foment a feeling we might call dread.

- Antidemocracy in Contemporary Times

- Reaching for the Democratic Ideal

- Applying Democracy in the Classroom

- Reflections on Solidarity

CHAPTER SEVEN

TEACHING ELLS AND THE DEMOCRATIC IDEAL

I AM NOT SURE WHEN OR why it happened, but at some point in this century, progressive educational writers and researchers stopped citing the work of Jane Addams. Jane Addams? Do not feel bad if her name is not familiar. In my opinion, her work is woefully under-appreciated, and I think that every U.S. history class should devote two weeks to studying Addams. She embodies everything that is good and thoughtful for those who work in the interests of immigrant children and their families.

Addams began what was then called a settlement house in Chicago in 1889, offering immigrant women and children a place to learn English, gain job skills, and attend learning clubs. For the next fifty years, Addams directed the Hull House while also serving as the president of the Women's International League for Peace and Freedom and founding the Immigrants' Protective League. Her tireless efforts won her the Nobel Peace Prize in 1931; she was the first American woman so honored.

Addams's work in direct assistance to immigrant families was guided by a clear and comprehensive theoretical
vision of social life (she did not call herself a social
worker but instead a sociologist). Many progressive
philosophers, John Dewey among them, based their own
work on Addams's views. Her general approach to philosophy was pragmatic feminism, a melding of pragmatic
ideals and feminist commitments.

Like her pragmatist colleagues, Addams believed that
philosophic questions about the essential nature of truth
and logic were interesting but that more compelling
questions came from how people came to agree on what
they *believed* to be true. Her pragmatism also compelled
her to answer philosophical questions in the reality of
human experience. I have a hunch that one of John
Dewey's most famous quotations from *Democracy and
Education* ("Education is the laboratory in which philosophic distinctions become concrete and are tested")
emerged from his conversations with Addams. Feminism, for its part, fueled her belief that women had been
subjugated in many aspects of modern life and that new
and creative ways of thinking about women were needed.
In fact, many credit Addams with the success of women's
suffrage, which came to pass in 1920.

In my view, Addams should serve as the role model for
ELD teachers who wish to connect their classroom work
to the wider social needs of ELLs. The following quote
from Addams is at once dated and strikingly modern:

> I know little Italian boys who joyfully drop their English
> the moment they are outside the school-room door; and
> others of them who are teaching the entire family and
> forming a connection between them and the outside
> world, interpreting political speeches and newspapers
> and eagerly transforming Italian customs into American
> ones. One watches the individual boy with great interest,
> to see whether he will faithfully make himself a transmit-
> ter and helper, or whether he will be stupidly pleased

with his achievements, and consider his examinations the aim of his life. I sometimes find myself nervously watching a young man or woman in a university in much the same way, and applying essentially the same test. I wonder whether his knowledge will in the end exercise supreme sway over him, so that he will come to consider it "a self-sufficing purveyor of reality" and care for nothing further, whether he will become, in the end, "school bound" with his faculties well trained for acquisition, but quite useless in other directions. (Addams 1899, 38–39)

Addams knew that immigrant students who were given the opportunities to learn English and gain knowledge of the United States could help their families integrate into their new culture. We might find her comment about transforming customs somewhat didactic, especially in our era when ethnic customs and identities are to be preserved at great cost, but she was absolutely correct in recognizing that immigrant families' customs would be altered by living in the United States. Furthermore, Addams believed that knowledge must be used for something beyond school, and she made every effort to let visitors to the Hull House know that knowledge should never lie inert. Knowledge moves justice forward.

What is also a bit quaint in Addams's writing is her faith in U.S.-style democracy, which she argued demands that we seek out diverse people and learn of their perspectives. This view may sound idealistic, but there is no denying the progressive's sometimes naïve belief in the power of democracy. Modern progressives such as Addams are aware of democracy's flaws but are not willing to give up on it.

ANTIDEMOCRACY IN CONTEMPORARY TIMES

Although I see great promise in the foundations of our democracy, I have been shocked at the patently undemocratic movements in the United States over the last

decade or so. For instance, Lou Dobbs, the host of a popular Fox News program, has devoted much of his show's
programming time to distorting the immigration "crisis": "This illegal alien crisis is one of the forces that is
putting extraordinary pressure on the Denver school district, where Hispanic students are dropping out of public
schools there in record numbers" (http://transcripts.cnn
.com/TRANSCRIPTS/0604/28/ldt.01.html). Disregard-
ing the contradictory nature of this statement (i.e., if the
students are dropping out, how can they be putting pressure on schools?), Dobbs has garnered a loyal following
by painting the so-called crisis in such stark terms. I have
watched (painful though it is) Dobbs's show for some
time, and he has never once interviewed an "illegal alien."
If he had, he would have most likely learned about a
young man in his twenties, schooled to the eighth or
ninth grade, from a rural state in central Mexico, who had
come to the United States to work. Co-opting the national identity? Designs on ruining a once-proud America? Ridiculous.

Dobbs's program builds on a long tradition of undemocratic immigrant bashing. In a comment familiar
to today, but made in 1911, a report by the Immigration
Commission stated bluntly that earlier northern and
western Europeans immigrated to the United States with
the intention of building a better country. These immigrants, the report argued, had a familiarity with democratic processes. The report went on to argue that recent
immigrants, who came from southern and eastern Europe, lacked experience with democratic life and had little intention of becoming active citizens (Ueda 1994). It

Think for a moment: Have you ever been confronted with blatant
hatred or disgust for immigrants? You may have felt it was a direct
attack on you and your students. How can you respond to this
attack? What if it came from within your school?

was argued that these recent immigrants were only interested in work.

If such a claim were true, then it is truly remarkable that the millions of immigrant families from Italy and Poland, for example, have now become fully enmeshed in the democratic lifeblood of the nation, which I take as evidence of the power of the democratic promise. I also think that it is safe to assume that recent immigrants to the United States will take the same path.

Public schools have been asked to be a primary democratizing agent.

REACHING FOR THE DEMOCRATIC IDEAL

U.S. public schools have been asked, for better or worse, to be a primary democratizing agent. In its highest ideal the school takes all children in, offers everyone an equal chance to succeed, and rewards those who work hard with a better life. Add to these challenges the goal of helping immigrants share in the social consciousness, and you have set the bar high indeed. Although we can easily lament the inequality of the public schools and point out the clear disparities in educational resources spent on recent immigrants and those on more established families, I find it heartening to note how often this broken and generally neglected system helps an ELL achieve beyond what his or her limited opportunities would suggest.

As teachers of ELLs, we are the vanguards for the initiation of our students into democratic life. Few other social institutions can do the job of the schools with regard to socializing youth and families into the rights and responsibilities of a democracy. Yet teachers can overplay the initiation, until it becomes thoughtless indoctrination and nationalism. As a PhD student, I was given the opportunity to supervise dozens of student teachers, many of whom completed their practicum in bilingual or ELD classrooms. On one of my visits to a school in Orange County, California, I ran across a teacher who heard that I was from the university and interested in

Cross-Reference See Book 1, Chapter 6 for discussion of teacher identity and democratic principles.

English learners. She sought me out with the intention of sharing her philosophy and invited me to her classroom. Every inch of wall space was devoted to some icon or iconic piece of U.S. history. The Pledge of Allegiance was displayed in six-inch letters so that her students could read and memorize it easily. Oversized copies of the Constitution and the Declaration of Independence, pictures of George Washington and Abraham Lincoln, and dozens of U.S. flags covered the classroom walls. She had, in effect, created a monument to U.S. patriotism in her classroom.

As I listened uncomfortably to her tell of her desire to create patriotic "Americans" of her fourth-grade immigrant students, I was reminded again that making unthinking nationalists could not be the goal of ELD teachers. Students would have to be introduced carefully into a democratic ideology, and in place of icons, they needed to be given genuine opportunities to understand U.S. political and social life. Fortuitously, I very soon found a pedagogical frame around which to organize my interest in helping my students learn the critical nature of living in a democracy and the special role required to gain participation and agency in a pluralistic society.

APPLYING DEMOCRACY IN THE CLASSROOM

As a doctoral student I took courses part-time so that I could continue teaching. At first, my motivation was financial: I simply could not pay for graduate school without my teaching job. But later I realized that staying in

Think for a moment: What artwork and posters adorn the walls of your own classroom? Have you ever done a careful analysis of those items to help determine if any of them could be a source of confusion for your students? Consult with a fellow teacher if there is anything you are unsure of.

the classroom while completing my program had a profound influence on both my learning and my teaching.
Two years into my graduate degree and six years into
teaching, I was growing more comfortable with the intense workload and learning daily how the very "theoretical" ideas in graduate school had immediate relevance to
ELD teaching. At this important point in my development as a teacher/scholar, my mentor Mary Poplin, who
always seems to find the trends in educational thought
about a decade before the rest of us, invited Paulo Freire
to the campus for a visit. I was lucky enough to be one of
several graduate students with whom he shared his
thoughts. Prior to his visit, I read his books, including
the now famous *Pedagogy of the Oppressed*. His conversations with Ira Shor, at the time in draft form and not yet
a book, were also very compelling to me. Fascinated by
the thought of a curriculum that emerged from student
knowledge and the overt political nature of his theory, I
began to consider ways that I might engage in a dialogic
and critical model of teaching and learning with my own
fourth-grade ELL students, though I quickly found that
the task was not easy. After all, Freire had taught adults
in Brazil, and Shor, whose work was at least situated in
the United States, worked with community college students on Staten Island.

As I considered how to create a critical teaching unit
(teachers like me think in units) for students, I recalled
the dialogic method that I distilled from many critical
teaching sources. First, I wanted to help my students
conduct a deconstruction of a **binary opposition**, a strategy of encouraging learners to examine critically a false
either/or construction, while recognizing the latent value
often placed on one side. As I further considered my options for the unit, I decided that social studies was a great
place to start. The books I had been given to use were
very old and dull, and the students groaned every time I
suggested we read them. What binary opposition, I
thought, could be worked to help students understand

Key concept
binary opposition

more about social studies? After weeks of consideration, I arrived at the notion of public versus private ownership. Ownership was a concept easily grasped by nine-year-olds ("That's *my* skateboard—I got it for Christmas"), and I believed I could help them understand more about democratic life in the United States by exploring what was owned by whom.

I began by inviting the students to create two categories, a T-chart list, of things that are privately owned and those publicly owned. Students first were drawn to objects such as houses, cars, their toys, and finally, schools. Yes, our school was publicly owned by all the people who lived within the school district. Everyone owned it, so no one could sell it, wreck it, or even buy it. People in the district could use it (clearly it was created to educate students) if they asked permission, because it was owned by all. After a new round of items on our list (I contextualized the list with illustrations for our beginning ELLs), one of the students mentioned sidewalks. Publicly or privately owned? I asked. Most agreed that sidewalks were owned by everyone. After creating our lists, I asked them which of these publicly owned things they wanted to study further, and sidewalks was the nearly unanimous reply.

I had secretly hoped that they would choose the school or a government building. Information on those topics was easier to find. Studying sidewalks was going to be a challenge; I guess I should have known the risks when I encouraged students to select the curriculum.

Think for a moment: Could you use the notion of private versus public ownership to begin a lesson in your own classroom? How could you do it? What other binary oppositions could be used in your classroom to engage students in learning about social studies?

Following the example of the critical teaching method I learned from Ira Shor, I created a presentation on sidewalks, which I asked them to critique. Had I covered the major points? What more did they want to know? Had I presented the information fairly? The students enjoyed offering suggestions about how I could have done better. I then divided the students into small groups in which their task was to think of as many questions about sidewalks as possible. I later assembled all the questions, and we prioritized them. We decided on several topics that we wanted to learn more about: (1) how are sidewalks made? (2) who decides where they go? (3) can you make someone get off the sidewalk in front of your house? and (4) who repairs them?

Knowledge is for action.

Now came the really challenging part for the teacher (me). With no ready-made instructional materials for teaching about sidewalks, it was up to me to develop a new curriculum. True, I wanted my students to investigate these questions for themselves, but it seemed too difficult to ask the students, for instance, to call the county maintenance department for information on sidewalk repair. I did find some information on the legal rights of people to assemble on sidewalks, but I had to modify these documents significantly before having them work in groups on this topic. I also researched how sidewalks are made and later brought in a wheelbarrow and showed the class how to mix concrete. We experimented with different ratios of mix to water, for instance.

With the critical teaching maxim "Knowledge is for action" in mind, I wondered where the students and I could take our burgeoning understanding of sidewalks. The answer came from one of the students who lived in the neighborhood around the school. Poorly chosen trees had been planted on several streets, and the roots had cracked and buckled the sidewalks so badly that roller skating and skateboarding had become impossible. He asked if we could fix the sidewalks, given our new knowledge of concrete mixing. I responded by saying that we probably could do that work, but that it would be a very big job, likely beyond our time, skill, and resources. But I did explain that as something publicly owned, sidewalks everywhere should be built and repaired to the same standard. It did not matter where you lived or how much money you had, your sidewalks should be as good as anyone else's. The students, as I had hoped, were growing in their capacity to see themselves as something other than a "subject" in a democracy (cf. Biesta 2006).

I then drove to a new housing development and took photographs of the beautiful sidewalks there. Most of the students immediately understood that even though their neighborhood was poor, their sidewalks should be up to standard. Who fixed the sidewalks? they asked. I had earlier found the county maintenance office number and phone, and it was quickly decided that a letter writing campaign should be launched. These letters, I told them, had to be written in a formal tone, with proper business letter formatting. They should be typed (i.e., word processed) and free of all errors. The conditions received wide agreement from the students.

With the letters completed and sent, the students began to receive replies and even phone calls from the county with apologies and plans for repairs. (The county had no idea the letters had come from fourth graders!) Realizing it probably was not fair to let the county maintenance officials feel bad for such a torrent of concern, I called the supervisor there, who was thankful for my explanation. He told me to share with the students that they would put in place a plan to replace as many of the cracked sidewalks as possible. By that summer, several of the most offending sections were repaired, and in the fall, my former students, now fifth graders, gleefully dragged me through the neighborhood and showed me each pristine, flat sidewalk.

I do not claim that helping nine-year-olds repair sidewalks is akin to the revolutionary learning that the critical theorists advocated, but it did give my students an introduction to equity in the public sphere. They and their parents pay sales and property taxes (if they rented, you can be sure the landlord accounted for these taxes in the lease). I am reminded of Leo Chavez's point: citizenship is not about legal definitions, but rather about participation in society (Chavez 2008).

I have had trouble replicating the success of that critical teaching "unit" on sidewalks but have since helped other teachers with their own efforts. The power of critical teaching with ELLs, however, is evident. The students in the class learned that even if their parents were undocumented, they had the same right to sidewalks of quality as more wealthy children. They learned how to write a business letter with a genuine purpose in mind. They learned the power of the *word*, and, more important, they understood at least one way to participate in democracy in a way that I think Jane Addams would have smiled upon.

I am reminded of Leo Chavez's point: citizenship is not about legal definitions, but rather about participation in society.

REFLECTIONS ON SOLIDARITY

ELD teachers will naturally have specific language goals for their students, and making the sounds of English will certainly be among them. What linguists call *phonological*

It often comes as a surprise to many people that undocumented workers have Social Security and Medicare taxes automatically withheld from their paychecks. But because most undocumented workers have fake ID numbers, they will never receive any of the benefits they are paying for. And because many do not file a tax return, they never receive a tax refund if they have overpaid. In fact, the Social Security Administration clearly understands that such workers are contributing an uneven share to the national "pot" and has named the funds the "earnings suspense file." It accounts for about 10 percent of the total dollars collected and grows by $50 billion each year.

accuracy is more commonly understood as speaking with a "foreign accent." Professional ELD teachers will endeavor for their students not only to use the correct syntax and word choice but also to "sound" like a native speaker. For teachers of young children, the sounds of a new language seem to come magically, and within a year or two, children who begin learning an L2 before age eleven or twelve almost always end up sounding like native speakers, irrespective of their native language. Thousands of research studies documenting this phenomenon (e.g., Yeni-Komshian, Robbins, and Flege 2002) have tried specifically to prove or disprove a theory known as the *critical period hypothesis. Research into a critical period for phonological accuracy has demonstrated without a doubt that if one begins learning a language before about age twelve, he or she is far more likely to sound like a native speaker than someone who begins learning a language after puberty (Oyama 1976). What makes this finding even more compelling is that it does not seem to matter how long they have been speaking the language. Sounding like a native speaker depends on when you began hearing and speaking that language, regardless of how many years of study.*

Focus point

In its most general form, the critical period hypothesis suggests that sometime after a certain age, typically around the onset of puberty, learning to make the sounds of a target language becomes much less likely. This common finding has fueled the growth of so-called accent reduction schools the world over, of which most are focused on helping ELLs sound as though they grew up in a suburban city in the midwestern United States. As ELD teachers, we have a responsibility to share with the non–language-teaching public why it is so hard to achieve native-like phonological proficiency. Furthermore, the public at large needs to understand that not sounding like a native speaker is unrelated to one's capacity for all other aspects of language.

Interestingly, though we have clear evidence of the critical period hypothesis with regard to phonology, we have little or no evidence for its effect on other features of L2 acquisition (e.g., syntax, semantics). In fact, a recent study (Hakuta, Bialystok, and Wiley 2003) examined immigrants in the U.S. Census data and found no evidence of a distinct critical age indicating a special time requirement for gaining English proficiency. (The study did not assess whether participants achieved phonological accuracy.)

I learned about the critical period for the sounds of a language many years ago as an undergraduate student in psychology, when I read a paper on birdsongs. The research suggested that if a male bird did not learn his particular mating song by a certain age, he would sing nonetheless, but that no female would recognize his song, and finding a mate would be unlikely—a sad fate indeed. It struck me that perhaps something similar is at work in humans, and for twenty years I wondered about it. As I studied evolutionary anthropology, I came to the belief that our capacity for acquiring the native sounds of a language with ease must have a social purpose.

For most of our history as a species, humans gathered in groups ranging in the hundreds, and it was very important to know who was part of your social group and who was not. Survival depended on sticking together, so it seemed to me that our inability to sound like a native speaker past adolescence had some value in creating solidarity. Coincidentally in the writing of this book, I came upon an article by Elizabeth Spelke and Katherine Kinzler (2007) that argues that our native language "accent" is a powerful marker for social identification. Spelke and Kinzler believe that the sound of the native language provides powerful information for social group membership even as early as infancy.

This artifact of our history seems to be saying something like, "Even if you can understand us, and we can understand you, we know by the way you sound that you are not one of us. You did not grow up among us." Of

Not sounding like a native speaker is unrelated to one's capacity for all other aspects of language.

course, judging people's belongingness by their native accent is always wrong, and I truly hope that no ELD teacher does so. But in the wider world, it helps the ELD teacher understand how important language is to social solidarity, and that we have to work hard to overcome our culture's limits on who is considered part of *us*. We are trying to overcome ten thousand years of history of making judgments about people based on the sounds of their native language.

Focus point

Native language creates a convenient but poor marker of social solidarity, and it is the job of ELD teachers to help our students and the wider society overcome this artifact we have used to identify outsiders. It is a feature of human development we need to leave behind for good. The sounds of language, while offering a clear indication of who is and who is not a native speaker, are irrelevant when it comes to true competence in a language. Solidarity must be reconfigured in our modern world, and one's native language should become a superfluous marker of group membership. If ELD teachers are doing their work, then each and every human language will be regarded as a gift from our collective past and the language learned first will become important but not necessarily more identifying than additional languages. Learning languages expands our social world and thus the people we might consider as one of us.

As I reconsidered the creation of new solidarity with people who may not look or speak like "us," it struck me that widening such a world must begin with a process at the level of the personal, the psychological. And my thoughts turned to the concept of caring, as it has been so richly explored by Nel Noddings (1984) and later by Angela Valenzuela (1999). Together their work has helped us redefine the essential student/teacher relationship. Because most teachers are not comfortable with saying that they "love" their students, at least not in the way they say they love their own children or their parents, and because most teachers are not comfortable describing their relationship with students as a cold and calculated business relationship ("I'm here to teach you. That's it"), our profession was in need of an entirely new way of thinking about our work. Noddings helped us to forge a new and sophisticated understanding of caring, one that has particular implications for ELD teachers, who, as givers of language and thus of the wider world, have a very special relationship with their students. As we explored earlier, ELLs are likely to view their teacher as more akin to a parent than as merely a teacher, and Noddings shows how caring and mothering have similar qualities when she writes, "Mothering is not a role but a relationship" (1994, 128). For the ELD teacher, the consequences of not caring for ELLs, of failing to recognize the caring relationship with her students, are disastrous.

Valenzuela, for her part, documents the lack of care shown to Mexican American students (many of whom were ELLs) who attended an overenrolled and largely dysfunctional high school. Not every teacher lacked a commitment to thoughtfully integrate students' cultural lives into the life of the school, but the manifold habits of the school convinced the students that it did not care. However, if they "cared" about their schooling (i.e., did exactly what the school told them to do), then the school would "care" about them. The premise and conclusion here must be reserved. It is our job as the adults in charge to first care about our students and then see what comes our way. In order to enrich our democracy, which I would argue serves to enlarge the solidarity of all people, the impulse to care must be the starting point.

The newest expression of Jane Addams's philosophical commitments comes in the work of Richard Rorty (although I hesitate to say if she would recognize her work in his). Rorty, who died in 2007, was claimed by

We are lucky to be at the intersection of language, culture, geopolitics, and initiation into democratic life.

the *New York Times* to be one of the most influential modern thinkers. As a pragmatist, he is a controversial figure in U.S. philosophy. He had no time for metaphysical questions and believed that language in the form of slogans, pithy truisms, or novels could guide humanity to a more united and peaceful world. He wrote:

> The right way to take the slogan "We have obligations to human beings simply as such" is as a means of reminding ourselves to keep trying to expand our sense of "us" as far as we can. That slogan urges us to extrapolate further in the direction set by certain events in the past—the inclusion among "Us" of the family in the next cave, then of the tribe across the river, then of the tribal confederation beyond the mounts, then of the unbelievers beyond the seas (and, perhaps last of all, of the menials who, all this time, have been doing our dirty work). This is a process which we should try to keep going. We should stay on the lookout for marginalized people—people whom we still instinctively think of as "they" rather than "us." We should try to notice our similarities with them. The right way to construe the slogan is as urging us to *create* a more expansive sense of solidarity than we presently have. The wrong way is to think of it as urging us to *recognize* such a solidarity, as something that exists antecedently to our recognition of it. For then we leave ourselves open to the pointlessly skeptical question, "Is this solidarity *real?*" (Rorty 1989, 196)

As ELD teachers, we do not stop to question the solidarity we are creating among and with our students. We just keep going. We get up in the morning and build community by teaching English. I think this type of modern pragmatism fits with the way many teachers think and act.

As teachers of English in the United States, we are taking the baton from the thousands upon thousands of teachers who have worked to help young people learn English and integrate into life in a new country, one with a clearly flawed and uncertain democracy, but one that probably offers more freedom and promise than their previous homes. We cannot fall into promoting an uncritical nationalism, which is always ill-advised, and we must battle against the racism and linguicism our students will no doubt face, but neither should we take for granted the life chances that the United States can offer its most recent arrivals. Our nation's public schools continue to play a key role in creating new citizens. We are most fortunate to have been invited to participate in this vast historical endeavor in which all our destinies are tied.

CONCLUSION

Focus point

As an ELD teacher (or teacher-to-be), you are responsible for introducing your students to the foundations of the democratic ideal. You must also keep an eye on the geopolitical trends in order to make predictions about who your future students will be. You will need to understand the culture of your students more deeply than a professional anthropologist as you help your students gently adapt to their new world without forsaking the old. Finally, you must be aware of some very subtle psychological factors that influence the teacher-student relationship as a result of language teaching. After some reflection, it appears that teaching English may be your easiest task.

For my part, I cannot imagine more compelling and rewarding work than that of ELD teachers. We are lucky to be at the intersection of language, culture, geopolitics, and initiation into democratic life. I hope that this book has shared my enthusiasm for teaching ELLs and that you will engage (or perhaps reengage) children and youth who very much need your guidance.

DISCUSSION QUESTIONS

1. As an ELD instructor, what do you see as your primary task in educating your students? Is it language, school culture, social skills, or perhaps American democratic ideals? Have you accepted the challenge that all of these may be your responsibility, and more?

2. Flip back through the book. Did you highlight, notate, or mark any special sections? What parts did you find most applicable to your daily instruction? What parts will you find useful as an advocate for your students outside of the classroom?

3. Where will you go next in your development as an ELD teacher? Language lessons? Guitar lessons? Singing lessons? Or perhaps more reading, some of which may be suggested in this book? Make yourself a list of next steps or goals.

4. Are you ready to share your inspired vision of what it means to be an ELD teacher? What will you say to others?

FURTHER READING

Dewey, John. 1897. "My Pedagogic Creed." *School Journal* 54: 77–80.
   It surprises me that more educators are not familiar with Dewey's short but powerful creed. The last line, "I believe that in this way the teacher always is the prophet of the true God and the usherer in of the true kingdom of God," should be enough to compel readers to it.
Johnston, Bill. 2002. *Values in English Language Teaching*. Mahwah, NJ: Lawrence Erlbaum.
   This book explores the moral principles inherent in teaching English. Johnston's compelling work provides multiple examples of the choices English-language teachers must make. It also provides an overview of the "English as linguistic hegemony" argument.
Knight, Louise W. 2005. *Citizen: Jane Addams and the Struggle for Democracy*. Chicago: University of Chicago Press.
   A superb retrospective of Addams's life that I hope will revive an interest in this very special figure in U.S. history.

REFERENCES

Addams, Jane. 1899. "A Function of the Social Settlement." *The Annals of the American Academy of Political and Social Science* 13, no. 3: 33–55.

Ainsworth, Mary D. Salter. 1969. "Object Relations, Dependency, and Attachment: A Theoretical Review of the Infant-Mother Relationship." *Child Development* 40, no. 4: 969–1025.

Alexander, Debbie, Sheila Heaviside, and Elizabeth Farris. 1999. *Status of Education Reform in Public Elementary and Secondary Schools: Teachers' Perspectives*. Washington, DC: U.S. Department of Education, National Center for Education Statistics.

Arnold, Jane. 1999. *Affect in Language Learning*. Cambridge: Cambridge University Press.

Ash, Doris, Kip Téllez, and Rhiannon Crane. 2009. "Objects and Science Instruction: The Special Case of the English Language Learner." In *Talking Science, Writing Science: The Work of Language in Multicultural Classrooms,* ed. Katherine R. Bruna and Kimberly Gomez, 269–288. New York: Routledge.

Baumann, Gerd. 1996. *Contesting Culture: Discourses of Identity in Multiethnic London*. Cambridge: Cambridge University Press.

Berthoff, Ann E. 1988. "Sapir and the Two Tasks of Language." *Semiotica* 71, nos. 1–2: 1–47.

Biesta, Gert. 2006. *Beyond Learning: Democratic Education for a Human Future*. Boulder, CO: Paradigm Publishers.

Bowlby, John. 1982. "Attachment and Loss: Retrospect and Prospect." *American Journal of Orthopsychiatry,* 52, no. 4: 664–678.

———. 1999. *Attachment and Loss*. New York: Basic Books.

Brown, Roger. 1973. *A First Language: The Early Stages*. Cambridge, MA: Harvard University Press.

California Legislative Analyst's Office (LAO). 2007. 2007–08 Budget Book: Education Analyses.

Caplan, Nathan S., Marcella H. Choy, and John K. Whitmore. 1991. *Children of the Boat People: A Study of Educational Success*. Ann Arbor: University of Michigan Press.

Capps, Randy, Michael Fix, Julie Murray, Jason Ost, Jeffrey Passel, and Shinta Herwantoro. 2005. *The New Demography of America's Schools: Immigration and the No Child Left Behind Act*. Washington, DC: Urban Institute.

Carrier, Karen A., and Alfred W. Tatum. 2006. "Creating Sentence Walls to Help English-Language Learners Develop Content Literacy." *Reading Teacher* 60, no. 3: 285–288.

Chavez, Leo R. 2008. *The Latino Threat: Constructing Immigrants, Citizens, and the Nation*. Stanford, CA: Stanford University Press.

Cho, Yung-Ho, and Jeong-Koo Yoon. 2001. "The Origin and Function of Dynamic Collectivism: An Analysis of Korean Corporate Culture." *Asia Pacific Business Review* 7, no. 4: 70–88.

Chomsky, Noam. 1959. "Verbal Behavior." *Language* 35, no. 1: 26–58.

———. 1968. *Language and Mind*. San Diego, CA: Harcourt Brace.

Clark, Eve. 1995. *The Lexicon in Acquisition*. Cambridge: Cambridge University Press.

Cohen, Y., and Marlene J. Norst. 1989. "Fear, Dependence and Loss of Self-Esteem: Affective Barriers in Second Language Learning Among Adults." *RELC Journal* 20, no. 2: 61–77.

Cragg, Michael Ian, and Mario Epelbaum. 1996. "Why Has Wage Dispersion Grown in Mexico? Is It the Incidence of Reforms or the Growing Demand for Skills?" *Journal of Development Economics* 51, no. 1: 99–116.

Crawford, James, ed. 1992. *Language Loyalties: A Source Book on the Official English Controversy*. Chicago: University of Chicago Press.

Cummins, Jim. 1986. "Empowering Minority Students: A Framework for Intervention." *Harvard Educational Review* 56, no. 1: 18–36.

Curran, Charles A. 1983. "Counseling-Learning." In *Methods That Work: A Smorgasbord of Ideas for Language Teachers*, ed. John W. Oller Jr. and Patricia A. Richard-Amato, 146–178. Rowley, MA: Newbury House Publishers.

Dapretto, Mirella, and Susan Y. Bookheimer. 1999. "Form and Content: Dissociating Syntax and Semantics in Sentence Comprehension." *Neuron* 24, no. 2: 427–432.

Dewaele, Jean-Marc. 2005. "Investigating the Psychological and Emotional Dimensions in Instructed Language Learning: Obstacles and Possibilities." *Modern Language Journal* 89, no. 3: 367–380.

Dewey, John. 1897. "My Pedagogic Creed." *School Journal* 54: 77–80.

Dörnyei, Zoltan. 2005. *The Psychology of the Language Learner: Individual Differences in Second Language Acquisition.* Mahwah, NJ: Lawrence Erlbaum.

Dörnyei, Zoltan, and Angi Malderez. 1999. "The Role of Group Dynamics in Foreign Language Learning and Teaching." In *Affect in Language Learning,* ed. Jane Arnold, 155–169. Cambridge: Cambridge University Press.

Enright, D. S., and M. L. McCloskey. 1988. *Integrating English: Developing English Language and Literacy in the Multilingual Classroom.* White Plains, NY: Addison Wesley.

Fishman, Joshua A. 1980. "Bilingualism and Biculturalism as Individual and as Societal Phenomena." *Journal of Multilingual and Multicultural Development* 1, no. 1: 3–15.

Flores, Lisa A. 2003. "Constructing Rhetorical Borders: Peons, Illegal Aliens, and Competing Narratives of Immigration." *Critical Studies in Media Communication* 20, no. 4: 362–387.

Freire, Paulo. 1995. *Letters to Cristina.* New York: Continuum.

Furman, Erna. 1982. "Mothers Have to Be There to Be Left." *Psychoanalytic Studies of the Child* 37: 15–28.

Galindo, René. 2004. "Newspaper Editorial Response to California's Post–Proposition 227 Test Scores." *Journal of Latinos and Education* 3, no. 4: 227–250.

Gándara, Patricia, Russell Rumberger, Julie Maxwell-Jolly, and Rebecca Callahan. 2003. "English Learners in California Schools: Unequal Resources, Unequal Outcomes." *Education Policy Analysis Archives* 11, no. 36: 1–54.

García, Ofelia, Jo Anne Kleifgen, and Lorraine Falchi. 2008. *From English Language Learners to Emergent Bilinguals.* New York: Teachers College Press.

Garza, Carmen Lomas. 2005. *Family Pictures.* San Francisco: Children's Book Press.

Gimenez, Martha E. 1997. "Latino/Hispanic—Who Needs a Name? The Case Against a Standardized Terminology." In *Latinos in Education: A Critical Reader,* ed. Antonia Darder, Rodolfo D. Torres, and Henry Gutiérrez, 225–239. New York: Routledge.

Guiora, Alexander Z., Benjamin Beit-Hallahmi, Robert C. L. Brannon, Cecelia Y. Dull, and Thomas Scovel. 1972. "The Effects of Experimentally Induced Changes in Ego States on Pronunciation Ability in a Second Language: An Exploratory Study." *Comprehensive Psychiatry* 13, no. 5: 421–428.

Gutierrez, Lorraine, Anna Yeakley, and Robert Ortega. 2000. "Educating Students for Social Work with Latinos: Issues for the New Millennium." *Journal of Social Work Education* 36, no. 3: 541–557.

Hakuta, Kenji, Ellen Bialystok, and Edward Wiley. 2003. "Critical Evidence: A Test of the Critical-Period Hypothesis for Second-Language Acquisition." *Psychological Science* 14, no. 1: 31–38.

Halliday, Michael A. K. 1975. *Learning How to Mean*. London: Edward Arnold.

———. 1979. "One Child's Protolanguage." In *Before Speech: The Beginning of Interpersonal Communication*, ed. Margaret Bullowar, 171–191. Cambridge: Cambridge University Press.

———. 1993. "Towards a Language-Based Theory of Learning." *Linguistics and Education* 5, no. 2: 93–116.

Hardin, Valentina Blonsky. 2001. "Transfer and Variation in Cognitive Reading Strategies of Latino Fourth-Grade Students in a Late-Exit Bilingual Program." *Bilingual Research Journal* 25, no. 4: 417–439.

Hauser, Marc. D., and Josh McDermott. 2003. "The Evolution of the Music Faculty: A Comparative Perspective." *Nature Neuroscience* 6, no. 7: 663–668.

Herrell, Adrienne L., and Michael L. Jordon. 2007. *Fifty Strategies for Teaching English Language Learners*. Upper Saddle River, NJ: Pearson.

Holzman, Matilda. 1984. "Evidence for a Reciprocal Model of Language Development." *Journal of Psycholinguistic Research* 13, no. 2: 119–146.

Huntington, Samuel P. 1991. *The Third Wave: Democratization in the Late Twentieth Century*. Norman: University of Oklahoma Press.

———. 2002. *The Soldier and the State: The Theory and Politics of Civil-Military Relations*. Cambridge, MA: Belknap Press.

Johnston, Bill. 2002. *Values in English Language Teaching*. Mahwah, NJ: Lawrence Erlbaum.

Kandel, William, and Emilio A. Parrado. 2005. "Restructuring of the U.S. Meat Processing Industry and New Hispanic Migrant Destinations." *Population and Development Review* 31, no. 3: 447–471.

Kenneally, Christine. 2007. *The First Word*. New York: Penguin.

King, Desmond S. 2000. *Making Americans: Immigration, Race, and the Origins of the Diverse Democracy*. Cambridge, MA: Harvard University Press.

Kloss, Heinz. 1977. *American Bilingual Tradition*. Rowley, MA: Newbury House.

Knight, Louise W. 2005. *Citizen: Jane Addams and the Struggle for Democracy*. Chicago: University of Chicago Press.

Krashen, Stephen. 1989. *Language Acquisition and Language Education*. Englewood Cliffs, NJ: Prentice Hall.

Landes, Ruth. 1965. *Culture in American Education*. New York: Wiley and Sons.

Li, Guofang. 2004. "Perspectives on Struggling English Language Learners: Case Studies of Two Chinese-Canadian Children." *Journal of Literacy Research* 36, no. 1: 31–72.

Lindholm-Leary, Katherine. J. 2001. *Dual Language Education*. Clevedon, UK: Multilingual Matters.

Loeffler, Melissa. 2005. *NCELA Fast FAQs*. Washington, DC: National Clearing House for English-Language Acquisition and Language Instruction.

Lorenzo-Dus, Nuria, and Patricia Bou-Franch. 2003. "Gender and Politeness: Spanish and British Undergraduates' Perceptions of Appropriate Requests." In *Género, Lenguaje y Traducción*, ed. José Santaemilia, 187–199. Valencia, Spain: Universitat de Valencia/Dirección Generalde la Mujer.

Lowe, Anne S. 1998. "Teaching Music and Second Languages: Methods of Integration and Implications for Learning." *Canadian Modern Language Review* 54: 218–238.

Mahler, Margaret S., Fred Pine, and Anni Bergman. 2000. *The Psychological Birth of the Human Infant: Symbiosis and Individuation*. New York: Basic Books.

McCafferty, Steven G. 2002. "Gesture and Creating Zones of Proximal Development for Second Language Learning." *Modern Language Journal* 86, no. 2: 192–203.

McMullen, E., and J. R. Saffran. 2004. "Music and Language: A Developmental Comparison." *Music Perception* 21, no. 3: 289–311.

Medina, Suzanne L. 1990. "The Effects of Music Upon Second Language Vocabulary Acquisition." Paper presented at the annual meeting of the Teachers of English to Speakers of Other Languages, San Francisco, March.

Meyer, Michael M., and Stephen E. Fineberg, eds. 1992. *Assessing Evaluation Studies: The Case of Bilingual Education*. Washington, DC: National Academy Press.

Mohan, Bernard, and Gulbahar Huxur Beckett. 2003. "A Functional Approach to Research on Content-Based Language Learning: Recasts in Causal Explanations." *Modern Language Journal* 87, no. 3: 421–432.

Nguyen, My Hang Thi. 2002. *The Impacts of Vietnamese-American Parents' Religious Values, Beliefs, and Practices on Their Children's Academic Performance*. Unpublished PhD diss., University of Houston.

Nichols, Patricia C., and Manuel Colón. 2000. "Spanish Literacy and the Academic Success of Latino High School Students: Code-Switching as a Classroom Resource." *Foreign Language Annals* 33, no. 5: 498–511.

Noddings, Nel. 1986. *Caring: A Feminine Approach to Ethics and Moral Education*. Berkeley: University of California Press.

Olsen, Laurie. 1997. *Made in America: Immigrant Students in Our Public Schools*. New York: New Press.

Orfield, Gary, Erica D. Frankenberg, and Chungmei Lee. 2003. "The Resurgence of School Segregation." *Educational Leadership* 60, no. 4: 16–20.

Orrenius, Pia M., and Madeline Zavodny. 2005. "Self-Selection Among Undocumented Immigrants from Mexico." *Journal of Development Economics* 78, no. 1: 215–240.

Ortega, Adolfo. 1991. *Caló Orbis: Semiotic Aspects of a Chicano Language Variety.* New York: Peter Lang.

Ortega, Lourdes. 2009. *Understanding Second Language Acquisition.* Oxford: Oxford University Press.

Oyama, Susan. 1976. "A Sensitive Period for the Acquisition of a Nonnative Phonological System." *Journal of Psycholinguistic Research* 5, no. 3: 261–283.

Parrish, Thomas, Maria Perez, Amy Merickel, and Robert Linquanti. 2006. *Effects of the Implementation of Proposition 227 on the Education of English Learners, K–12: Findings from a Five-Year Evaluation.* San Francisco: American Institutes for Research.

Passel, Jeffrey. 2007. "Unauthorized Immigrants in the United States: Estimates, Methods, and Characteristics." OECD Social, Employment, and Migration Working Papers No. 57, available online at http://www.oecd.org/dataoecd/41/25/39264671.pdf (accessed August 30, 2008).

Pearson, Greg. 2006. *Ask NCELA No. 1: How Many School-Aged English-Language Learners (ELLs) Are There in the U.S.?* Washington, DC: National Clearinghouse for English Language Acquisition and Language Instruction.

Pulido, Laura. 2007. "A Day Without Immigrants: The Racial and Class Politics of Immigrant Exclusion." *Antipode* 39, no. 1: 1–7.

Pullum, Geoffrey K. 1991. *The Great Eskimo Vocabulary Hoax and Other Irreverent Essays on the Study of Language.* Chicago: University of Chicago Press.

Quine, Willard. V. O. 1964. *Word and Object.* Cambridge, MA: MIT Press.

Ramirez, J. David, Sandra D. Yuen, Dena R. Ramey, and David J. Pasta. 1991. *Longitudinal Study of Structured English Immersion Strategy, Early-Exit, and Late-Exit Transitional Bilingual Education Programs for Language-Minority Children.* San Mateo, CA: Aguirre International.

Robinson-Stuart, Gail, and Honorine Nocon. 1996. "Second Culture Acquisition: Ethnography in the Foreign Language Classroom." *Modern Language Journal* 80, no. 4: 431–449.

Rolstad, Kellie, Kate Mahoney, and Gene V. Glass. 2005. "The Big Picture: A Meta-Analysis of Program Effectiveness Research on English Language Learners." *Educational Policy* 19, no. 4: 572–594.

Roney, M. W. 1994. "Moving Beyond the Tricks of the Trade, or Using Common, Everyday Items as Realia." *Hispania* 77, no. 2: 298–300.

Rorty, Richard. 1989. *Contingency, Irony, and Solidarity*. Cambridge: Cambridge University Press.

Ryding, Karin C. 1993. "Creating a Learning Community: Community Language Learning for the Nineties." In *Georgetown University Roundtable on Languages and Linguistics*, ed. James E. Alatis, 137–147. Washington, DC: Georgetown University Press.

Sanchez, George. J. 1993. *Becoming Mexican American: Ethnicity, Culture, and Identity in Chicano Los Angeles, 1900–1945*. New York: Oxford University Press.

Schachter, Paul, and Fe T. Otanes. 1972. *Tagalog Reference Grammar*. Berkeley: University of California Press.

Schumann, John H. 1976. "Social Distance as a Factor in Second Language Acquisition." *Language Learning* 26, no. 1: 135–143.

———. 1990. "Extending the Scope of the Acculturation/Pidginization Model to Include Cognition." *TESOL Quarterly* 24, no. 4: 667–684.

Scribner, Sylvia, and Michael Cole. 1973. "Cognitive Consequences of Formal and Informal Education: New Accommodations Are Needed Between School-Based Learning and Learning Experiences of Everyday Life." *Science* 182, no. 4112: 553–559.

Searchinger, Gene. 1995. *The Human Language*. Series. Equinox Films, Inc.

Shady, Michele, and Louann Gerken. 1999. "Grammatical and Caregiver Cues in Early Sentence Comprehension." *Journal of Child Language* 26, no. 1: 163–175.

Shor, Ira. 1987. *Critical Teaching and Everyday Life*: Chicago: University of Chicago Press.

Shor, Ira, and Paulo Freire. 1987. *A Pedagogy for Liberation: Dialogues on Transforming Education*. Westport, CT: Bergin and Garvey.

Siegel, Jeff. 1997. "Using a Pidgin Language in Formal Education: Help or Hindrance?" *Applied Linguistics* 18, no. 1: 86–100.

Skutnabb-Kangas, Tove. 2000. *Linguistic Genocide in Education, or Worldwide Diversity and Human Rights?* Mahwah, NJ: Lawrence Erlbaum Associates.

Snyder, Jerry. 1985. *Children's Songs for Guitar*. Miami, FL: Warner Bros. Music.

Spelke, Elizabeth S., and Katherine D. Kinzler. 2007. "Core Knowledge." *Developmental Science* 10, no. 1: 89–96.

Stewner-Manzanares, Gloria. 1988. "The Bilingual Education Act: Twenty Years Later." http://www.ncela.gwu.edu/pubs/classics/focus/06bea.htm (accessed September 5, 2008).

Storr, A. 1993. *Music and the Mind*. New York: Ballantine Books.

Swarns, Rachel L. 2007. "U.S. Considers Broader Visa Plan for Iraqis." *New York Times*, February 14.

Téllez, Kip. 1998. "Class Placement of Elementary School Emerging Bilingual Students." *Bilingual Research Journal* 22, nos. 2–4: 279–295.

———. 2002. "Multicultural Education as Subtext." *Multicultural Perspectives* 4, no. 2: 21–25.

———. 2004. "Preparing Teachers for Latino Children and Youth: Policies and Practice." *High School Journal* 88, no. 2: 43–54.

———. 2008. "What Student Teachers Learn About Multicultural Education from Their Cooperating Teachers." *Teaching and Teacher Education* 24: 43–58.

Téllez, Kip, and Marilyn Estep. 1997. "Latino Youth Gangs and the Meaning of School." *High School Journal* 81, no. 2: 69–72.

Téllez, Kip, Susan Flinspach, and Hersholt C. Waxman. 2005. "Resistance to Scientific Evidence: Program Evaluation and Its Lack of Influence on Policies Related to Language Education Programs." In *Language in Multicultural Education,* ed. R. Hoosain and F. Salili, 57–76. Greenwich, CT: Information Age Publishing.

Téllez, Kip, and Hersh C. Waxman. 2006. *Preparing Quality Educators for English Language Learners: Research, Policies, and Practices.* Mahwah, NJ: Lawrence Erlbaum Associates.

Toohey, Kelleen, and Elaine Day. 1999. "Language-Learning: The Importance of Access to Community." *TESL Canada Journal* 17, no. 1: 40–53.

Tufte, Edward. R. 1990. *Envisioning Data.* Cheshire, CT: Graphics Press.

U.S. Department of Commerce and U.S. Census Bureau. 2000. "America Speaks: A Demographic Profile of Foreign-Language Speakers for the United States." http://www.census.gov/population/www/socdemo/hh-fam/AmSpks.html (accessed October 7, 2007).

Ueda, Reed. 1994. *Postwar Immigrant America: A Social History.* Boston: Bedford Books.

Valdés, Guadalupe. 1997. "Dual Language Immersion Programs: A Cautionary Note Concerning the Education of Language-Minority Students." *Harvard Educational Review* 67, no. 3: 391–429.

———. 2001. *Learning and Not Learning English: Latino Students in American Schools.* New York: Teachers College Press.

Valenzuela, Angela. 1999. *Subtractive Schooling: US-Mexican Youth and the Politics of Caring.* Albany: State University of New York Press.

Vernez, Georges, and Kevin F. McCarthy. 1996. "The Costs of Immigration to Taxpayers: Toward a Uniform Accounting Framework." *Population and Environment* 18, no. 1: 9–36.

Vigil, James Diego. 1988a. *Barrio Gangs: Street Life and Identity in Southern California.* Austin: University of Texas Press.

———. 1988b. "Group Processes and Street Identity: Adolescent Chicano Gang Members." *Ethos* 16, no. 4: 421–445.

Vygotsky, L. 1978. *Mind in Society*. Cambridge, MA: Harvard University Press.

Weaver, Constance. 1988. *Reading Process and Practice: From Socio-Psycholinguistics to Whole Language*. Portsmouth, NH: Heinemann Educational Books.

Wells, Miriam J. 1996. *Strawberry Fields: Politics, Class, and Work in California Agriculture*. New York: Cornell University Press.

Wiesner, David. 1999. *Sector 7*. New York: Clarion Books.

Wilson, Edward O. 1998. *Consilience: The Unity of Knowledge*. New York: Knopf.

Yeni-Komshian, Grace H., Medina Robbins, and James E. Flege. 2002. "Effects of Word Class Differences on L2 Pronunciation Accuracy." *Applied Psycholinguistics* 22, no. 3: 283–299.

Zukowski-Faust, Jean. 1997. "What Is Meant by Realia?" *AZ-TESOL Newsletter* 18, no. 1: 9.

Sources for some of the statistics I cite:

U.S. Department of Education, NCES. National Household Education Survey (NHES), 1999 (Parent Interview Component) U.S. Department of Education's Survey of the States' Limited English Proficient Students and Available Educational Programs and Services, 1991–1992 through 2000–2001 summary reports; state publications (1998–1999 data); enrollment totals from the National Center for Educational Statistics Core of Common Data, 1998–1999 through 2004–2005; FY 2002 Consolidated State Applications for State Grants under Title IX, Part C, § 9302 of the Elementary and Secondary Education Act (P.L. 107-110); 2004–2005 Consolidated State Performance Reports; and additional 2002–2005 data reported by state. August 2006.

U.S. Department of Education's Survey of the States' Limited English Proficient Students and Available Educational Programs and Services, 1991–1992 through 2000–2001 summary reports; state publications (1998–1999 data); enrollment totals from the National Center for Educational Statistics Core of Common Data, 1998–1999.

INDEX

accent, native, 157–158

accent reduction schools, 156

acquire/learn, 65–66, 82; behaviorism for, 66; environment on, 67; Krashen's theory of, 69–70; language, 66–67

acronyms: misinterpreting, 4; use of, 2–5

action, knowledge for, 153

Addams, Jane: immigrant work by, 145–147, 155, 159; Nobel Peace Prize for, 145; pragmatic feminism of, 146

Africa, 62–63

African American, 105

amnesty law, 1986, 15–16

animal communication, 70

animal learning stations, 124–125

Arabic, 13

argot, 122

Arizona, 34; Proposition 227 in, 86

Asian American, 5

attachment theory, 137–138; extreme results of, 135; as instinctual, 134–135; key concept of, 134; language and, 134–137; responsive caregiver in, 134

Attenborough, David, 75

Baumann, Gerd, 32

behaviorism, 66

bicultural/multicultural, 50

bilingual education, 106–107; civil rights in, 89–90; cognitive rationale for, 91–92; debates on, 85–90; early/late-exit, 92, 93–94; effect size for, 95–96; ELD default for, 86; exit criteria in, 93; focus point of, 92; history of, 88–90; key concept of, 92; in Massachusetts, 88; politics of, 88–90, 98; research on, 93–98; in San Francisco, 88–89; teacher shortages for, 89; teaching skills for, 94; timing of transition to instruction in, 92

Bilingual Education Act, 1984, 89

Bilingual Immersion Evaluation Project, 93–95; limitations of, 94

bilingual language use, 100

bilinguals, emerging, 4

binary opposition: deconstruction of, 151; key concept of, 151; social studies project of, 151–155

Bookheimer, Susan, 81

border security, 37

Bowlby, John, 134–135

brain: language capacity for, 80; word knowledge in, 81

Brower, Jonathan, 136

Brown, Roger, 91
Buchanan, Pat, 39–40
Burton, Virginia Lee, 72
Bush, George W., immigration policy of, 18

California, 86; ELL population of, 33–34
Caplan, Nathan, 53
caring, 158–159; by schools, 159
Carrier, Karen, 81
CCL. *See* community language learning
Census, U.S., 32–33, 157; on Latinola/Mexican Americans, 36–37; reification of, 37–38
Center for Immigration Studies (CIS), 14
Chaplin, Charlie, 74
Chavez, Leo, 38–39, 155
chicken, cut up, 42
Chinese, 54, 102; ELLs, 33; orthographic symbol system of, 63
Chomsky, Noam, 66–70, 78
Choy, Marcella, 53
CIS. *See* Center for Immigration Studies
citizenship: in democracy, 155; as participation, 155
Civil Rights Act, 1964, Title VII, 88–89
Clark, Eve, 122
classroom, safety of, 133
Clever Hans, 70
code-switching, 99–100, 103, 106; key concept of, 99
Cohen, Y., 140
Collection of The Mexican Museum, 57
community language learning (CCL), L2 learning with, 138–140
comprehensible input, 69
Constitution, 150
content, conceptual foundations of, 71, 80, 112–113
creoles, 23–26; Latino youth gangs as, 26; linguistic, 24

critical period hypothesis: focus point of, 156; for L2, 156–157; for phonology, 156–157
cultural/typological distance, 139
culture, 20–26, 161; changes in, 32, 37–38, 46–47, 58; comparisons of, 44–45; ELD teachers learning, 6, 26, 58–59, 98, 106; European-American, 44–45; focus point of, 26; home, 25–26, 48–49; L2 for, 23–24; language v., 23, 25, 35–36; Latin American, 39; Mexican American, 46–47; realia for learning, 125; recognition of, 31; reification of, 32, 45; routine practice of, 47–48; school, 21–23, 31, 48–50; space, 25; teacher/student, 21–22, 31; U.S., 37–38, 74; Vietnamese, 50–56; Western, 39. *See also* bicultural/multicultural; second culture
Cummins, Jim, 89–90, 91
Curandera (Faith Healer), as sacred, 57p
Curran, Charles A., 138–140
curriculum: customized, 128; student developed, 151–155

Dapretto, Mirella, 81
Day, Elaine, 115
Declaration of Independence, 160
democracy, 76; anti-, 147–149; caring in, 159; for ELLs, 17; focus point of, 161; school goals for, 149–155; schools for, 16–17; as social consciousness, 17
Democracy and Education (Dewey), 146
Department of Education, U.S., 93
Dewaele, Jean-Marc, 138–139
Dewey, John, 17, 146
Diaz, Porfirio, 16
Discussion Questions, 27, 59, 82, 107, 129t, 143, 162
Dobbs, Lou, 148
documents, false, 15–16
Dörnyei, Zoltan, 142

early/late-exit, 92, 93–94; criteria for, 93
earnings suspense file, 155
ELD. *See* English-language development
ELD teachers, 21–23, 31, 47, 95, 97;
animal communication use for, 70;
child learning recreated by, 78; code-
switching by, 99–100, 106; cultural
learning for, 6, 26, 58–59, 98, 106;
culturally- bound materials for, 56–
58; customized curriculum for, 128;
democracy introduction by, 149–
150; education of, 6–7; ELL's
statistics for, 30; focus point for, 29,
78, 99, 101, 120; gestures for, 64–
65; immigration opportunities for,
12–13; knowledge, extra for, 26–27;
knowledge, four arenas of, 7–26;
knowledge of, English, 8; language
acquisition knowledge for, 61–62,
70; learning about languages, 5–6,
7–8; linguistic capacity of, 87;
linguistic "placeholder" by, 71;
meaningful lessons by, 78–80;
misunderstanding by, 56–58; music/
guitar learning for, 115–116; native
language instruction and, 87, 90,
106–107; native language learning
by, 9, 98–99; nonverbal
communication by, 9–10; parenting
by, 131–132, 134–137, 159; refugees
helped by, 6; reification awareness by,
38; resources for, 7; responsibilities
of, 161; solidarity by, 160–161;
student affiliations fostered by, 142,
143; student relationship with, 102,
131–134, 143, 158–159, 161; terms
of endearment by, 101–103; trends
anticipated by, 30; two kinds of
learners for, 140–141;
underprepared, 6–7; video/camera
equipment for, 127. *See also* bilingual
education
ELLs. *See* English-language learners
endearment, terms of, 101–103

English, 8, 103–106; global use of, 1–2;
models for, 103; SVO syntax of, 67
English as a second language (ESL),
term of, 2–3
English-language development (ELD),
3; bilingual default of, 86; content-
based, 112–113; effect size for, 95–
96; focus point of, 3; music/singing
for, 113, 114–118; research on, 93–
98; student achievement pressure in,
113; teaching, 5–6, 95. *See also* ELD
teachers
English-language learners (ELLs), 4;
comprehension factors for, 126;
democracy for, 17; focus point of,
141–142; historical comparisons of,
33; home/school connections for, 59;
hosts of, 34; Latinola's/Mexican-
American's as, 4–5, 34–35; in May 1
marches, 19–20; meaningful
instruction for, 78–80; numbers of,
6–7, 32–34; poverty of, 41; previous
knowledge of, 29; school for, 16–17;
solidarity among, 142; statistics of,
30–36; teacher attachment by, 131–
134; Vietnamese as, 33–35; view of
themselves, 30–31. *See also* students
English teaching, term of, 3
"Eskimo" myth, 35–36
ESL. *See* English as a second language
ethnic/racial, 17, 34, 161; balance, 37–
38; statistics, 36; terms for, 4–5
Europe, immigration patterns in, 13
European-American, 57; culture, 44–45
experience boxes, 123–124

Field Museum, Chicago, 124
Figure 5.1 language teaching core, 111f
filial piety, 54–55
"Fishing in the Americas," 124
Florida, 34
focus point, 3, 20, 22, 26, 29, 63–64, 78,
92, 99, 101, 110, 114, 119, 120, 123,
132, 137, 141–142, 156, 158, 161

"The Fox," 117
Fox News, 148
Frege, Gottleib, 80
Freire, Paulo, 109, 151
French, 13
French Haitian language, 24
Freud, Anna, 131
Freud, Sigmund, 131
Further Reading, 27–28, 59–60, 83,
    108, 129–130, 144, 162

Garza, Carmen Lomas, 56–57
gender equity, 48
generalizations, scientific, 43, 58–59; of
    Latinolas/Mexican Americans, 44–
    47; understanding from, 46–47; of
    Vietnamese, 53
geopolitics, 161; immigration on, 12–
    13, 15–16
Gerken, Louann, 76
German, 13; language instruction, 88
gestures, 70, 82; L1 beginning with, 71;
    language development with, 64–65;
    meaning with, 64–65; teaching
    strategy of, 64–65
Gimenez, Martha, 38
Glass, Gene, 95
Google, 126
graphic organizers, 125–126
Greek, 1
guest worker program, 18
Guthrie, Woody, 116–117

Halliday, Michael, 10; language
    functions theory of, 100
Harris Educational Loan Center, 124
Hauser, Marc, 114
Hispanic: population of, 37–38; term of,
    4–5
Hmong: American, 43; ELLs, 33
Holling, Holling C., 74–75
Homo sapiens, 63
Hop on Pop (Seuss), 119
Hull House, 145–146, 147

Huntington, Samuel, 39
Hussein, Saddam, 13

illegal immigrant, term of, 30
illegal worker, term of, 14
Illinois, 34
The Immigrant (Chaplin), lesson for, 74
Immigrants' Protective League, 145
immigrant workers, 15–16, 42–43,
    145–147, 155, 159; crisis of bashing,
    148–149; fear of, 40–41; focus point
    of, 20; poverty of, 41; school
    challenge of, 149; U.S. nation of, 18
immigration, 12–13, 146, 147; Bush's
    bill on, 18; to Europe, 13; historical
    comparisons of, 40–41; of Mexican
    Americans/Latinolas, 38–43; political
    stance against, 41–42; reasons for,
    42; short/long term costs of, 41;
    stories of, 74; Univision news on, 20
Immigration Bill: defeat of, 18–19;
    opposition bill to, 19
Immigration Commission, 1911, 148–
    149
individuation, 136
"infant-directed talk." *See* "motherese"
international border, 20
Internet, 126
Inuit language, 35–36
Iraqis: refugees from, 13; to
    Syria/Sweden, 13
iTunes, 75

justice, knowledge moved by, 147

Keats, Jack Ezra, 72
Kenneally, Christine, 66
Kentucky, ELLs in, 34
key concept, 17, 40, 76–77, 91, 92, 99,
    122–123, 134, 151
Kinzler, Katherine, 157
koiné language (common language), 1–2
Korean, SOV syntax of, 67
Korean American, 43

Korean ELLs, 33
Krashen, Stephen, 79–80, 112; acquisition/learning theory of, 69–70

L1. *See* language acquisition, first (L1)
L2. *See* second-language teaching
L.A. Morgan Elementary, 105
labeling, 2–5
Lambert, Wallace, 89
language, 7–12; acquisition, 10–11, 61–62, 66–67, 69–70, 138–140; additive/subtractive, 89–90; attachment theory and, 134–137; capacity for, 63–64, 80, 87; communication through, 6; communication without, 9–10; communicative competence in, 110; culture v., 23, 25, 35–36; deep structure of, 91–92, 100; desire to understand for, 71; developmental process of, 3, 4; developmental/structural learning of, 10, 70, 94; emotional development for learning, 138–139, 141; exposure to, 70; focus point of, 63–64, 110, 114; high intelligence with, 11–12; human origins of, 62–66; interactional function of, 100–103; learning, 10, 158; learning about, 5–8, 10; learning through, 10; music links with, 114–115; in schools, 33; Separation-Individuation theory for, 136; similarities of all, 67; specific syntax of, 67–68; three-part understanding of, 10; understanding/use of, 62; vocalizations for, 64. *See also* gestures; language fluency; *parole* (individual speech acts); speech, human
language acquisition, first (L1), 69, 74, 75–76, 111–112; emotional bonds for, 132; gestures beginning, 71; meaning in, 78, 80; objects of learning for, 120–123; prosody for,

76–77; psychological processes of, 133–134. *See also* "motherese"; native languages
language fluency, 110
language-free materials, 71–76; democracy in, 76; mime for, 74; silent movies for, 73–75; wordless books as, 72–73
language-reduced teaching strategies, 9–10
language teaching program, four features of, 97
langue (collective knowledge of language), 91–92
Latin, 1
Latinola: community growth of, 31; ELLs as, 33, 34–35; generalizations of, 44–47; immigration history of, 38–39; portraits of, 36–43; term of, 5; threat of, 38–43; traits/dispositions of, 44. *See also* Latino youth gangs
Latino youth gangs, 25–26; as creoles, 26; pidgin cultural frame of, 25–26; slang of, 25
Lau v. Nichols, 88–89
learners, independent, 131, 139, 141; balance for, 135
learning, accuracy/analysis, 110–111, 140
learning, cooperative, 142
learning, fluency/use, 110, 113, 140–141
learning, formal/informal, 119–120
LEP. *See* limited English proficient
lianas, paper airplane lesson on, 75
limited English proficient (LEP), 4, 89
Lincoln, Abraham, 150
lingua franca (Frankish), 1–2
linguicism, 161; key concept of, 17
linguistic genocide, 90
linguistic "placeholder," 72–73; for ELD teachers, 71
linguistics, iceberg theory of, 91–92

linguistic safety, 137–138
The Little House (Burton), 72
Lucas, George, 68

Macbeth (Shakespeare), 68
Magnolia Pictures, 75
Mahler, Margaret, 135–137
Mahoney, Kate, 95
Malderez, Angi, 142
marches, May 1, ELLs in, 19–20
McDermott, Josh, 114
McMullen, E., 114–115
meaningful instruction, 76; of algebra,
    78–79; by ELD teachers, 78–80; for
    ELLs, 78–80; gestures in, 64–65; in
    "motherese," 77–78
meat packing: foreign born workers in,
    42–43; labor pool for, 42–43. *See also*
    immigrant workers
Medicare taxes, 155
Mexican American, 5, 43, 45–47, 105;
    ELLs, 34–35; generalizations of, 44–
    47; immigration history of, 38–39;
    lack of care for, 159; portraits of, 36–
    43; Spanish dialect of, 102; terms of
    endearment for, 101–102; threat of,
    38–43; traits/dispositions of, 44;
    U.S. census reports on, 36–37
The Mexican Museum, Collection of,
    57
Mexico, 42; economic crisis in, 14–16;
    ELLs from, 4–5; unemployment in,
    13–14
Michael Halliday's Language Functions
    and Tasks, 100t
mime, 74
Monitor Model, 69
"motherese," meaning in, 77–78
mothering, 131, 159. *See also* parenting
movies, silent: for adult ELLs, 73–75;
    students creating, 74; topics of, 73–
    74
multiglossic, 8
multilinguals, 99–100, 103

music, 128; classroom songs of, 116–
    118; languages links with, 114–115
My Hang Thi Nguyen, 54

nationalists, 150, 161; indoctrination by,
    149–150
National Research Council report, 94
native languages, 4, 24–25; accent, 157–
    158; as "bootstrap," 93; in CA/AZ,
    86; ELD teacher learning forms of, 9,
    98–99; focus point of, 158;
    instruction in, 85–90, 106–107; L2
    with, 90, 92; language output in, 69–
    70; loss of, 1–2; for solidarity, 158;
    syntax of, 68. *See also* bilingual
    education
Natural Approach, tenets of, 112
Netflix, 73
Neurath, Otto, 23
New York, 34
New York Times, 160
Nguyen, My Hang Thi, 54
Nickel Creek, 117
9/11, 37
Nocon, Honorine, 25
Noddings, Nel, 158–159
Norst, Marlene, 140
North American Free Trade Agreement,
    14
North Carolina, ELLs in, 34

Ohanian, Susan, 118–119
Orrenius, Pia, 16
orthographic symbol system, 63
ownership, private/public, 152–153; of
    schools, 152; of sidewalks, 152–155

Paddle to the Sea (Holling), 74–75
parenting, by teachers, 131–132, 134–
    137, 159
parole (individual speech acts), 91
Pedagogy of the Oppressed (Freire), 151
Peter and the Wolf (Magnolia Pictures;
    on iTunes), 75

phonological accuracy: difficulty of, 156; solidarity with, 155–156, 157–158; younger children with, 156

Piaget, Jean, 67

pictographs/petroglyphs, 63

pidgins, 23–26; cultural midpoint of, 24; Latino youth gangs as, 25–26; slaves as, 24

"Pizza Song," 117–118

The Pledge of Allegiance, 150

polyglot, 8

Poplin, Mary, 151

populism: key concept of, 40; in U.S. politics, 39–40

The Private Life of Plants (Attenborough), 75

Proposition 227, 86–87; effects of, 96–97

prosody, 76–77; context with, 77; key concept of, 76–77

Quine, Willard, 121–122

rapprochement: focus point of, 137; L2 learning with, 138–139; as psychological birth, 137; successful, 136–137; unsuccessful, 137

realia, 128; classroom collecting of, 123–124; for culture, 125; focus point of, 123; key concept of, 122–123; for L2, 122–125

refugees, 6, 12–13; from Iraq, 13

regulation, as access, 17

reification: census data for, 37–38; of cultures, 32, 45; of Huntington, 39

religious traditions, 57–58

rhymes, 118–119; focus point of, 119

Robinson-Stuart, Gail, 25

Rolstad, Kelly, 95

Roney, M. W., 123

Rorty, Richard, 159–160; on solidarity, 160

Ryding, Karin, 138

Saffran, J.R., 114–115

"Sapir-Whorf" hypothesis, 36

de Sassure, Ferdinand, 91

schools, 37p, 113, 161, 162; in CA, 19; caring, 159; culture of, 21–23, 48–50; democratizing agent of, 16–17, 149–155; expectations for, 22–23; focus point of, 22; immigration challenge of, 149; L2 in, 69; languages in, 33; limitations of, 26; marginalizing, 48; on May 1 marches day, 19–20; point of reference for, 23; public ownership of, 152; reform of, 48; segregated, 104–106; teacher/student cultures in, 21–23, 31

Schumann, John, 23–25

Scott, Judith, 80

SDAIE. *See* specially designed academic instruction in English

second culture: acquiring, 47–50, 53, 56, 59; effort for, 48; friendship for, 51, 53, 56; personal desire for, 50; sharing story of, 50–56; student conversations for, 49; understanding of, 49–50

second-language teaching (L2), 3, 82, 111–112, 141, 156–157; adults, 73–75, 140; community language learning with, 138–140; comprehensible input for, 69; content lesson before, 71; culture for, 23–24; emotional bonds for, 132; focus point of, 132; form/function for, 110, 113; grammar-translation method for, 110; images/graphics for, 125–127; language output in, 69–70; learner growth stages for, 139; music for, 114–115; native language with, 90, 92; natural acquisition of, 69–70; objects of learning for, 120; pidginized, 24, 25–26; psychological processes of, 133–134; realia for, 122–125; in schools, 69; Separation-

Individuation theory for, 137–140; social distance for, 23–24; two kinds of, 140–141; younger children for, 81, 156

Sector 7 (Weisner), 72

seed dispersal, 75

SEI. *See* structured English immersion

Sendak, Maurice, 72

Sensenbrenner, James (R-WI), 19

sentences: "cloze," 81; communicating, 81; context of, 80–81, 125; forming exercise, 109; syntax for, 68; walls, 81

Separation-Individuation theory, 136–137; L2 learning with, 137–140; language/cognitive abilities of, 136

Seuss, Dr., 119

Shady, Michele, 76

Shakespeare, William, 68

Shor, Ira, 151, 153

Skinner, B.F., 66

The Snowy Day (Keats), 72

social consciousness: democracy as, 17; ELLs/families sharing, 17

social distance, 23–24

Social Security Administration, 155

Social Security cards, 15

solidarity: by ELD teachers, 160–161; among ELLs, 142; native languages marking, 158; phonological accuracy for, 155–158; Rorty on, 160

Somalia war, settlement agreements from, 12

South Carolina, ELLs in, 34

SOV/SVO/VSO, 67

Spanish language, 5, 25, 103–106; Mexican American dialect of, 102; students learning, 103; U.S. speakers of, 32–33

specially designed academic instruction in English (SDAIE), 3

speech, human, 82; cognition and, 11; as a consequence, 64; development of, 11; fundamentals of, 11

Spelke, Elizabeth, 157

Star Wars (Lucas), 68

statistics: on ELLs, 30–36; ethnicity, 36

stereotypes, 43, 46–47

strawberries: labor intensive, 15; technology/distribution of, 15

structured English immersion (SEI), 3

students, 21–23, 31, 49, 113; affiliations of, 72–73, 142–143; name for, 3–4; teacher relationship with, 102, 131–134, 143, 158–159, 161; terms of endearment for, 101–103

SVO/SOV/VSO. *See* syntax

"The Swimming Song," 117

syntax: computer programming language, 68; different patterns of, 67; of native languages, 68; of poets, 68; rhythm and, 115; for sentences, 68

Tatum, Alfred, 81

teaching, dialogic/critical, 151–155; knowledge/action in, 153

technology, 128

Texas, 34

Texas Instruments calculators, 79

Thanksgiving, sacred part of, 58

"This Land is Your Land" (Guthrie), 116–117

Toohey, Kelleen, 115

Tufte, Edward, 126

two-way programs, 103–106; challenges to, 104; positive social interactions from, 104–106; reintegration by, 103–106

undocumented workers, 40–41; agribusiness and, 14–16; legal status for, 18; march by, 19–20; taxes of, 155; teaching children of, 17

United States, 161; Census, 32; cheap labor for, 13–14, 15–16; culture, 37–38, 74; foreign-born people in, 40–41; immigration policy of, 12, 18; Iraqi visas to, 13; politics, 39–40; population of, 31. *See also* Census,

U.S.; European-American;
geopolitics; nationalists
Unz, Ron, 85–86, 93, 97–98

Valdes, Guadalupe, 104
Valenzuela, Angela, 158–159
Verbal Behavior (Skinner), 66
Vietnamese: Buddhist influence on, 55;
children's duties of, 54; Confucian
ideology for, 52, 53–55; cultural
understanding for, 50–56; education/
knowledge for, 54–55; ELLs, 33, 34–
35; filial piety of, 54–55;
generalizations of, 53; learning
motivations for, 55; "model
minority" of, 52; proverbs of, 54;
resettlement for, 12; study of, 53–55;
terms of endearment for, 102–103
Vigil, James Diego, 25
vocabulary instruction, 73, 80
VSO/SVO/SOV, 67
Vygotsky, 132

Wainwright, Loudon III, 117

Washington, George, 150
Washoe, 70
weightlifting, 51–52
Weisner, David, 72
Welsh, VSO syntax of, 67
Where the Wild Things Are (Sendak),
72
Whitmore, John, 53
Wilson, Edward O., 11
Wirth, Louis, 20–21
Women's International League for Peace
and Freedom, 145
women's suffrage, 146
Word and Object (Quine), 121
word consciousness, 80
wordless picture books, 72–73
word order. *See* syntax
word walls, 81
work permits, 15

"Yoda speak" website, 68
YouTube, 75

Zavodny, Madeline, 16

ABOUT THE AUTHOR

Kip Téllez is Associate Professor in the Education Department at University of California—Santa Cruz. Prior to joining UCSC in 2000, he taught elementary and high school in east Los Angeles county. His instructional focus has always been on teaching English-language learners. An interest in educational linguistics led him to earn his PhD at Claremont Graduate University in Claremont, California. After graduate school, he began his first academic position at the University of Houston, where he taught courses on methods and theories of second language education, while also working to initiate two-way dual immersion programs in the Houston/Galveston area. At UCSC he has continued his research on language teaching and learning, while also teaching the English Learning Development courses in the Masters/Credential program. He is currently serving as the chair of the Education Department.

Combining his interests in English-language teaching with teacher education, he has published articles in journals such as the *Journal of Teacher Education, Teaching and Teacher Education,* and *The Bilingual Research Journal.* He also published an edited book (with Hersh Waxman) in 2006 titled, *Preparing Quality Educators for English Language Learners.*